DATE DUE

SEP 0 6 2015	
SEP 1 2 2015 RF	
OCT 0 3 2015	
NOV 1 4 2016	
JUN 1 5 2017	

BRODART, CO.   Cat. No. 23-221

Mrs. Lee's
Rose Garden

Center Point
Large Print

**This Large Print Book carries the
Seal of Approval of N.A.V.H.**

Mrs. Lee's Rose Garden

THE TRUE STORY OF THE FOUNDING OF ARLINGTON

CARLO DEVITO

CENTER POINT LARGE PRINT
THORNDIKE, MAINE

This Center Point Large Print edition
is published in the year 2015 by arrangement with
Cider Mill Press Book Publishers LLC.

The text of this Large Print edition is unabridged.
In other aspects, this book may vary
from the original edition.
Printed in the United States of America
on permanent paper.
Set in 16-point Times New Roman type.

ISBN: 978-1-62899-614-2

Library of Congress Cataloging-in-Publication Data

DeVito, Carlo.
 Mrs. Lee's rose garden : the true story of the founding of Arlington /
Carlo DeVito. — Center point large print edition.
 pages cm
 Summary: "The poignant, personal, and unbelievably true story of Mrs.
Robert E. Lee and General Montgomery Meigs, and the founding of the
Arlington National Cemetery, in the midst of America's greatest
struggle—the Civil War"—Provided by publisher.
 ISBN 978-1-62899-614-2 (library binding : alk. paper)
 1. Arlington National Cemetery (Arlington, Va.)—History—19th century.
   2. Arlington House, the Robert E. Lee Memorial (Va.)
   3. Lee, Mary Randolph Custis, 1807–1873—Homes and haunts—
      Virginia—Arlington County.
   4. Lee, Robert E. (Robert Edward), 1807–1870—Homes and
      haunts—Virginia—Arlington County.
   5. Meigs, Montgomery C. (Montgomery Cunningham), 1816–1892.
   6. Soldiers' bodies, Disposition of—Virginia—Arlington County—
      History—19th century.
   7. United States—History—Civil War, 1861–1865—Casualties. I. Title.
F234.A7D48 2015
975.5´295—dc23

                                                          2015012210

This book is dedicated to the memory of Mrs. Mary Anna Randolph Custis Lee, General Robert E. Lee, and Brigadier General Montgomery C. Meigs, and to all those that gave their "last full measure" in the service of this great nation.

And to Joseph Rue, the only grandfather I ever knew and loved, a veteran of World War II and a member of the greatest generation, so much like those who survived the Civil War—two of the greatest generations this nation has ever known.

"I never saw the country more beautiful, perfectly radiant. The yellow jasmine in full bloom and perfuming the air; but a death-like stillness prevails everywhere."

—Mary Custis Lee, to her husband, Gen. Robert E. Lee, CSA, Spring, 1861

CONTENTS

AUTHOR'S NOTE

This is a small story. That said it took a long time to come together.

Like any good story, or any good true story, it is one filled with small twists of fate that many readers, if found in fiction, would accuse the writer of seeming far-fetched or unrealistic.

This is not a history of Arlington National Cemetery. The history of our national cemetery is too long, too complicated, and too big to be told even remotely well in such as short a space as this. However, this is meant to be a small, personal, intimate story, with all the grandeur of a Greek tragedy, involving three accomplished people who lived their lives on the nation's stage.

The expert might point to stories I may have left out from this period, especially those of Salena Gray and James Parks, who were the real keepers of Arlington during the war. Unfortunately, their amazing and powerful personal histories and contributions in more featured rolls did not dovetail well with the current narrative, and a literary decision was made to excise their larger stories from the text. Few know the real debt of gratitude that the nation owes to these two people, and their involvement making history. They certainly deserve their own book.

Neither is this meant to serve as a complete biography of any of the three characters. Each has been re-examined by historians in the intervening decades, and there is no doubt countless new generations will re-examine their motives and actions. Lee and Montgomery have both been the subjects of numerous and large, multi-volume biographies. I must say that I find it discouraging that Meigs's contributions to our nation are not more celebrated. His career certainly deserves more consideration. He was a colossal presence in Washington in those days, and for good reason. He was an engineer of the first rank, unshakable in honesty, and driven to excess. His accomplishments should be more noteworthy. Lee's reputation speaks for itself. Complicated but still highly regarded by many. His decision, even 150 years or more later, is still the stuff of legend and conjecture. There is no doubt had he led the Union Army, as was intended, the war might have turned out much differently. But that too is another book.

As with any story of this type, there were generations who followed, distant relatives who added or detracted from the true history of what really happened. Sometimes fighting through these differing viewpoints are the toughest decisions a writer has to face.

Regardless, there was no attempt on my part to paint any of these three people a villain. The Civil

War was a complicated time. As the exploration of these three lives illustrates, friendships were made and stressed, beliefs were shattered and reinforced, loyalties put to the test.

Ultimately, their story ends up creating the national cemetery many Americans know and revere today. A place of great honor and sacrifice, a hallowed ground far more sacred than any words could ever make it so. This story is, as it should be, a salute to them.

PROLOGUE:
AMERICAN ACROPOLIS

The George Washington Parke Custis Mansion could be seen from almost anywhere in Washington city (as it was commonly referred to in those days, just before and after the Civil War), if you were looking westward from the downtown. The low rise of scattered buildings allowed a clear view of the giant columns that sat atop the hill across the Potomac: an American Acropolis watching over the region, one of the most dominant architectural edifices of the age. Long before D.C.'s other memorials were built, save the Washington Monument, the mansion at Arlington was one of the most recognized buildings in the region, and the Custis family was among the country's elite.

In the days before the war the mansion stood as a proud tower, a symbol of the nation's recent but great past, celebrating the man known to Americans as the Father of Our Country in grand style. The image of the building was often seen in newspapers, magazines, books, and prints. It was a place of prestige. Army officers, politicians, foreign dignitaries, and notable families alike were thrilled with the opportunity of an invitation to visit the mansion and to have an audience with

George Washington Parke Custis, stepgrandson and adopted son of George Washington, and to see the personal belongings of the nation's first president on display at Arlington. Custis was a consummate storyteller and showman, as entertaining as he was fascinating. His mansion was both a living memorial to George Washington and a beloved home for his family, including his daughter, Mary Anna Custis Lee, and her husband, General Robert E. Lee, who lived there for thirty years.

But the war had come and its dark and long reach had shadowed the land with pestilence and sorrow. And Arlington was no exception.

East view of the Arlington House portico.

By the end of the Civil War, death had cast a pall over the grounds and the mansion alike. Its reputation, in northern eyes, had already been sullied by Lee's traitorous turn, transforming it into a symbol of the general's treason and the southern states' secession. Now the countless boys and men he had slaughtered were being bedded down for eternity on his own grounds. The mansion hovered over the city like a ghost, a sad Golgotha, a daily, haunting reminder to the capital's denizens of the war's toll and the painful times in which they now found themselves. If sunlight had seemed to have perpetually shined on it in the days before the war, it now appeared dull and shabby, perpetually gray.

Robert E. Lee had fled Arlington years earlier, but he was well aware of what was going on at his former home. He wrote to his oldest daughter, Mary Custis Lee, in the last years of battle about the sufferings and privations of the war and the loss of Arlington:

"Having distributed such poor Xmas gifts as I had to those around me, I have been looking for something for you. I send you some sweet violets that I gathered for you this morning while covered with dense white frost that glistened in the bright sun like diamonds and formed a broche of rare beauty and sweetness, which could not be fabricated by the expenditure of a world of money. Yet how little it will purchase. But see how God provides for our pleasure in every way. May he guard and preserve you for me, my dear daughter. Among the calamities of war the hardest to bear perhaps is the separation of families and friends.

"Your old home if not destroyed by our enemies has been so desecrated that I cannot bear to think of it," he continued. "I should have preferred it to have been wiped from the earth, its beautiful hill sunk, its sacred trees burned rather than to have been degraded by the presence of those who revel in the ill they do for their own selfish purposes."

Many family members had made discreet visits to the old estate and passed back their commentary. This only fueled the Lees' homesickness and anger. Eventually, Mary Custis Lee, now thirty years old, went to the old estate while visiting friends in Georgetown after the war in late 1865. She wrote to her mother:

> We proceeded along a perfect road through a Country so changed that had I not known where I was I should have never identified it in the world. Not one single tree, not a bush, is standing on either side of the road. The heights from the river . . . are lined with fortifications & barracks & freedmans [sic] villages & back in the Country as far as the eye can reach the perfect desolateness extends. Where the Arlington tract commences

large placards are stuck over both sides of the road "Government Farms—Do Not Trespass" . . . On the Height the graveyard commences & extends almost to the little stream . . . The vegetable garden with its old brick wall & ivy looked just the same, the only thing that did . . . The flower garden is entirely altered, made smaller in every way . . . surrounded by a white paling . . . Round the paling were the row of graves of which you have heard. The front looked very desolate, all grown up with church mint & aspens & ailan thus . . . Not saying who I was, I was not allowed to enter many of the rooms . . . I went into the parlour, in which nothing was standing but the old sideboard, with broken doors . . . One of the mantels was also broken . . . I was forbidden to enter Papa's office . . . Upstairs I was permitted to go into my own dressing room "to see the view." There was nothing in it, nor the hall. I saw several of the servants in the distance but not wishing to be recognized did not speak to them. Thornton . . . Cornelius . . . & Dandridge I think & Robert. The grave-yard commences from the road as it descends the hill & stretches out . . . acre after acre . . . I returned that way over the long bridge to see as much as I could &

had I not been so unwell I would have gone over again. It was a very trying visit, more painful even than I had expected . . . It was a beautiful bright nice day and the view was lovely but the whole face of the country so utterly changed that turning my back on the house I could have scarcely recognized a feature of it.

Mary Anna Randolph Custis Lee, Mary's mother, could only clutch the letter and cry.

The dining room at Arlington House.

Mary Anna Custis Lee.

CHAPTER I

THE ROSE OF ARLINGTON

The young Mary Anna Randolph Custis walked contemplatively in the gardens not far from Arlington House, the mansion her father had built. She had loved the gardens of the estate from the time she was a little girl and had learned from her mother how to take care of flowers and tend her own beds.

She walked the gravel paths that divided the

large level plot south of the mansion. The garden's paths formed an ornate, looping design, cutting the beds into odd shaped but organized patterns. Now she passed through the large wooden arbor at the center of the garden that was thick with yellow jasmine and honeysuckle. Her father, George Washington Parke Custis, had laid out the garden many years before. Over the years, the responsibility for its care was assumed by her mother, Mary Lee Custis: when they reached young adulthood each of the four Custis daughters was given a small plot on which to cultivate her favorite flowers.

"Mary's earliest memories were of this hillside," wrote Custis biographer John Perry. "Her parents had begun the garden beside the house before she was born, and from the time she could hold a hoe, she had worked there, cultivating camellias, hyacinths, honeysuckle, gardenias, lilies, morning glory, dogwood and roses." The gardens at Arlington held magical memories for her. "Mary Custis enjoyed gardening as much as her mother always had. She lovingly tended the flowerbeds of her mother's rose arbor on the south lawn, its paths as familiar to her as her own room."

Roses were everywhere. Mrs. Custis loved the Cherokee rose in particular, a flower native to southern China and Taiwan and down through to Laos and Vietnam. An evergreen climbing shrub that reaches heights of up to thirty feet and boasts large, pure-white petals and a bristly stem, *Rosa laevigata* was first introduced to the United States in Georgia. In the early part of the 1800s, it became all the rage due to its powerful and pleasant fragrance, which was popular among ladies of the day.

Mary grew to love the Cherokee rose her mother adored and would cherish it until her own old age. While she shared a love of gardening with her mother, there were other pursuits in her life that were somewhat forward-thinking for her time. Young Mary Custis was already her own person and had been for as long as anyone could remember. She was not only distinct in her desires from her mother, but also from other young girls of her age.

"As Mary began the transition from girl to young lady, she revealed characteristics that confirmed her to be very much her father's daughter. Her conversation and the quickness with which she learned revealed a keen intellect," wrote Perry. "She had a gift for languages, and before her student years were over, she was reading French, Greek, and Latin. Arithmetic, which her father also struggled with in college, held little interest for her."

The Custises were avid readers, often reading aloud in the family rooms on the first floor works by Sir Walter Scott, Benjamin Disraeli,

Jane Austen, the Brontë sisters, Nathaniel Hawthorne, and others.

Living at the Arlington estate itself was a huge benefit to Mary. As historian Elizabeth Brown Pryor wrote, "Her most notable education . . . came through exposure to America's greatest personalities at her father's estate."

The Arlington mansion had a strong connection to important figures in American history. A Greek revival estate overlooking the Potomac River and the National Mall in the nation's capital, Arlington was built on the orders of Mary's father, George Washington Parke Custis, and designed by George Hadfield, an English architect who had also worked on the Capitol building in Washington. Arlington was built at a high point on a 1,100-acre estate that Custis's father, John Parke Custis, had purchased in 1778. It was the home of an impressive collection of George Washington memorabilia that Custis had amassed over the years, including furniture, the general's sword, assorted silverware and dinnerware, as well as Washington's personal papers and clothes and the command tent that the president had used at Yorktown.

"Custis also had a rich store of anecdotes about his grandparents," wrote Pryor, "and people traveled considerable distance to hear his reminiscences. As a result, Mary grew up conversing with leaders such as John Marshall and the Marquis de Lafayette."

Young Mary supplemented her historical and political education with a strong religious devotion. Her mother, "descended from Virginia's notable families, was a lady of unusual sympathy—a 'woman in a thousand' wrote one admirer. Strongly religious, she taught her daughter the importance of spiritual values and the need to live them out. Early in the 1820s Mary Custis helped form a remarkable coalition of women who hoped to eradicate slavery."

There was no denying Mary Anna Randolph Custis's absolute interest in the beauties of nature. She wrote in her notebook in February 1823, "Taste may be defined as the power of receiving pleasure from the beauties of nature and art. None are devoid of this faculty. Nothing that belongs to human nature is more universal than the relish of beauty of one kind or another, of what is orderly, proportioned, grand, harmonious, new, and sprightly. . . ."

Like her father, Mary loved to draw and paint. While he painted grand canvases with allegorical scenes, normally with General George Washington as the central figure, as a teenager Mary preferred to render flowers in black and white and then bring them to life with watercolors. "Her ability soon far surpassed her father's, though her pictures were never exhibited publicly," wrote Perry.

Though Mary had a deep appreciation of beauty, she herself was never considered a beauty.

She had inherited her father's sharp nose and chin. Nor did she ever put on the air of a Southern belle. However, "She captivated those around her. Her charm, wit, manners, thoughtfulness, and vivacity made her a popular guest, and she was constantly surrounded by friends and admirers," reported Perry.

An observer once remarked that her fun-loving personality and cheerfulness "combined to make her a toast in any social gathering in which she might be. She enjoyed society and was as popular in Washington as she was in Virginia." Already, at the age of sixteen, "she was the girl the crowd gathered around at parties: a wit, a painter . . . she fairly radiated the charms and graces of a woman worthy of her patrician and patriotic lineage, charms and graces that were becoming evident to every eligible bachelor in the District of Columbia and others besides."

"You would love this sweet modest girl, so humble & gentle with all her classical attainments. She has wit & satire too, when they are required," her aunt Eleanor "Nelly" Parke Custis Lewis wrote to a friend. "There are few worthy of her I think."

Indeed, Mary attracted a number of admirers, most notably the young, ambitious Sam Houston.

Born in Rockridge County, Virginia, to a family of Scotch-Irish descent, Sam Houston was a mentee of Andrew Jackson and a veteran of the

War of 1812, in which he had performed bravely and been injured. He later studied for the bar, and in 1818 Houston was appointed as the local prosecutor in Nashville. He was also given a command in the state militia. In 1822 Houston was elected to the U.S. House of Representatives for Tennessee where he served from 1823 to 1827.

In 1825, the dynamic congressman set his sights on young Mary Custis. He was thirty-two and in the mind to marry, he had told friends.

"Congressman Houston crossed the Potomac to pay his respects to Miss Custis a number of times. He dined with the family, talking politics with Mr. Custis and paying special attention to Mary. He wrote her poetry and courted her resolutely," wrote Perry. Mary was unmoved. In turn, she spurned other suitors as well.

"Mary was, evidently, an accomplished flirt. One of her chums teased her in 1825 about the 'mischief you are making upon the unfortunate youths around you,' exclaiming, 'praywhat have you done with poor Mr. Carter—Mr. Lloyd—Mr Lee & . . . a dozen or so swains who seem to be dying with the prevailing Love fever of the day,'" reported historian Elizabeth Brown Pryor.

During the summer of 1827, Mary visited Kinloch, in Fauquier County, the estate of her distant cousin Edward Carter Turner. Like the Custis family, Carter was also related to the Lee family. That summer Robert E. Lee had taken his first leave from West Point in two years, and he spent part of his time off at Kinloch. Robert and Mary had been acquainted with each other since childhood, but it was that summer at Kinloch that cemented their close bond.

Robert was lean, trim and athletic. He dressed in his uniform, and she thought he looked splendid. A great many girls flocked to this dark-haired, dark-eyed, dashing young man. But Mary, who had steeled her heart from so many suitors, was falling in love.

"In 1830, with the death of William Henry Fitzhugh, her mother's adored brother, Mary Custis underwent a profound transformation. Stunned at her uncle's inexplicable demise, she began to embrace evangelical religion," wrote Pryor. "For years her mother had followed the teachings of the Second Great Awakening, with its emotional surrender to a just, but inscrutable, God and rejection of transient worldly pleasures. For Mary Custis, this was the beginning of a spiritual quest that would become the guiding priority of her life, giving her an aspiration and emotional independence apart from domestic concerns." As Pryor pointed out, "Now she agonized over her willful nature and asked God to lead her away 'from pride, selfishness, indolence.'

"So it was that two spirits came together in the summer of 1830, both buffeted by loss and uncertainty, one homeless and unsettled, the other committed to pursuing a new and demanding path. When weather and water halted the operations at Cockspur Island, Lieutenant Lee was granted a furlough, and he chose to spend it in the company of his kin in northern Virginia," wrote Pryor.

And so in 1830, Mary Custis strolled through the gardens of Arlington, admiring her mother's Cherokee roses, and thought of Robert E. Lee.

*Stratford Hall Plantation,
birthplace of Robert E. Lee.*

CHAPTER 2
ROBERT E. LEE

Robert E. Lee was a dashing figure in 1830. He was adored by women and admired by men—although it was known by other cadets that he should not be crossed.

Lee was born at Stratford Hall Plantation in Westmoreland County, Virginia. He was the son of Major General Henry "Light-Horse Harry" Lee III, who later became governor of Virginia, and his second wife was Anne Hill Carter. His birth date has traditionally been recorded as January 19,

1807, but according to the historian Elizabeth Brown Pryor, "Lee's writings indicate he may have been born the previous year."

The Lees were one of Virginia's most distinguished families. Henry Lee I, grandfather of Henry Lee III, was a prominent Virginian colonist of English descent. His second cousin Richard Lee I, Esq., "the Immigrant," originally arrived in Virginia from England in the early 1600s. Robert's mother grew up at Shirley Plantation, one of the most elegant homes in Virginia.

Shortly after Robert's birth, however, the Lee family fell on hard times. Robert's father, a tobacco planter, suffered severe financial reverses from failed investments and was put in debtors' prison in 1809. A year later, following his release, Harry and Anne Lee moved with their five children to a small house in Alexandria, Virginia. But Lee's luck continued to decline. A staunch opponent of the War of 1812, he was with Alexander Contee Hanson, his friend and editor of the Baltimore newspaper *The Federal Republican*, on July 27, 1812 during an attack by a pro-war mob opposed to the paper's stance against the war. Lee, Hanson, and two dozen others took refuge in the newspaper's offices. Harry and the rest of the men surrendered themselves to Baltimore city officials the next day and were jailed. Laborer George Woolslager led a mob that forced its way into the jail, took the confined men by force, and beat and tortured them for almost three hours. All were severely injured. One man, James Lingan, died.

Lee suffered extensive injuries to his head, face, and internal organs, and his speech became slurred. Lee later sailed to the West Indies in an effort to recuperate from his injuries, but his health remained precarious, and in 1818 he decided to return home. He died on March 25, 1818, at Dungeness, on Cumberland Island, Georgia. The American fleet stationed near St. Mary's buried Lee with full military honors.

Throughout the time he was separated from his family, Lee only mentioned Robert once in a letter. But if his father was absent in his life, his mother became everything. Left to raise six children alone, Anne Lee doted on Robert, putting enormous effort into his schooling and development. To her, he was a special child, beautiful, and smart. Warm and outgoing, he made friends easily and showed restraint in his personal demeanor at all times.

Anne Lee's family was often supported by her uncle William Henry Fitzhugh, who allowed the Lees to stay at Ravensworth, his home in Fairfax County. In 1824, Fitzhugh wrote to the Secretary of War, John C. Calhoun, urging that Robert be given an appointment to the United States Military Academy at West Point. Lee entered West Point in the summer of 1825.

West Point was overseen by engineer officers at the time, and so Lee and his classmates studied engineering. Cadets were not permitted leave until they had finished two years of study. In 1827, the first year that he was allowed leave, he chose to spend some of that time with Mary Custis. Lee finished second in his class and did not earn a single demerit in his four years. In June 1829, he was commissioned a brevet second lieutenant in the Corps of Engineers.

While awaiting his assignment, Lee returned home to Virginia to visit his mother. She was dying.

"The newly graduated honor student became her full-time nurse. With no pull toward the pleasures of celebrating with companions of his own age, he gravitated naturally to his mother's bedside. What else could mean as much to him?" wrote biographer Clifford Dowdey. "The product of her stifled dreams, he was what he was because of her. Each intuitively understood the other, and he understood that part of himself lay dying. It was told that her dark eyes followed him whenever he left the room, and her gaze remained on the door until he came back in. In those last hours he was to Anne Carter Lee the hum of her days on earth." Anne Carter Lee died at Ravensworth on July 26, 1829.

Many years later, he returned to that home, an old man with a gray beard, and lingered in the doorway of what had once been her room, saying,

"Forty years ago I stood in this room by my mother's deathbed. It seems now but yesterday."

Robert then left for Georgia, where he was assigned to assist the lead engineer in building a fort on the Savannah River's Cockspur Island. His friend, Jack Mackay, a fellow West Pointer, lived in nearby Savannah. The two spent much time together, and Robert ingratiated himself with the Mackay family.

Though he squired Jack's sister Eliza to many events, his heart had already turned northward. He enlisted his sister to help him write to Mary to begin wooing her. His earliest attempts at winning her via correspondence show an awkwardness unusual to him. They were clumsy. He even attempted a poem, "Robert to Miss Polly" (one of Mary's nicknames). The poem lamented the fact that Polly had so many suitors.

> That I alas must be of those
> Who dare not meet such charms as hers

But with her ever sharp wit, Mary responded,

> Tell him that feint heart never won
>   fair lady . . .
> None but the brave deserve the fair.

It was in the summer of 1830 that their relationship grew more serious. He wooed her with ferocity. He flattered her. He brought her flowers. He wrote to her constantly. They read books together in the parlor of Arlington. They walked and rode the grounds of the great estate that overlooked Washington.

One night Robert read aloud to the family. Mary's mother suggested she fetch Robert something to drink. "As she stopped over the Mount Vernon sideboard to cut a piece of fruit cake, she felt Robert's arm slip around her waist. Both startled and pleased, she whirled to face him," described Perry.

"Molly, will you be my wife?" Robert asked. She happily assented. Mary's mother gave the couple her blessing immediately, but Mary's father hesitated. She would be marrying a soldier with no fortune, and he knew the lifestyle she was accustomed to. He eventually gave in, however. There was no point in arguing; he had raised a spoiled, willful daughter, and he knew it was useless to resist.

It was around this time, on July 4, 1830, that "something miraculous happened that brought her faith to a new and profoundly deeper level," wrote Perry. "That day a new light shone on Mary and led her to a fresh expression of her holy place in God's creation." This spiritual reawakening was an important turning point in her life.

Robert had to return to Savannah. And the

two began a stream of letters back and forth. "He spoke of his delight in her person, of his longing, and his desperate loneliness. The stack of love letters he left are among his most agreeable, crackling with sexual tension, filled with irreverent pokes at the military, and always seasoned with his disarming humor," opined Pryor.

The two were wed at Arlington on June 30, 1831. It was a magnificent affair, one of the events of the season. The mansion was ablaze with light and flowers, and carriages of all types lined the drive, ushering in important figures from Virginia and Washington. Afterwards, minstrels played Virginia reels deep into the night as ladies and gentlemen danced and whirled.

But reality quickly settled in. Robert was a lieutenant and was stationed in July 1831 at Fort Monroe. Mary moved with him to officers' quarters in the fort. It was a huge change from life at Arlington. She made friends with other officers' wives, but times were tense. Nat Turner had led a slave uprising, and the fort became crowded with more military personnel in the event of another rebellion. They did not return home to Arlington until Christmas.

For the next few years Mary and Robert traveled back and forth from his post to Arlington. But then he received new orders. The Mississippi River needed redirection, especially around the port of St. Louis, and he and another officer would be sent to redirect the river's powerful waters. In this adventure, he would meet a man with whom he would eventually be involved for the rest of his life.

The young, dashing Robert E. Lee.

Montgomery C. Meigs was a formidable engineer, and a product of his Puritan ancestry.

CHAPTER 3

MONTGOMERY C. MEIGS

Born in Augusta, Georgia in May 1816, Montgomery C. Meigs was the son of Dr. Charles Delucena Meigs and Mary Montgomery Meigs. Dr. Meigs was a nationally known obstetrician and professor of obstetrics at Jefferson Medical College and the son of Josiah Meigs, who had attended Yale with such classmates as future creator of the dictionary, Noah Webster, and American Revolutionary War general and politician Oliver Wolcott, and later became president of the University of Georgia. Montgomery's mother, Mary, was from a distinguished family. She was the granddaughter of a Scottish clan from Brigend (with somewhat distant claims to a baronetcy) that emigrated to America in 1701.

The Meigs family was wealthy and well connected, and Charles was an avid supporter of the Democratic Party. Young Montgomery received schooling at the Franklin Institute, a preparatory school for the University of Pennsylvania, where he learned French, German, and Latin, and studied art, literature, and poetry. Meigs had an extremely good memory, and his father instilled in him a sense of duty and a desire to pursue honorable causes from a young age. He enrolled at the University of Pennsylvania when he was only fifteen years old and was one of the top students in his class.

The Meigs family had extensive ties to the military and to West Point. Caught up in the nationalistic fervor of the time, Montgomery Meigs wished to serve in the army. Through family connections, he won an appointment to

West Point in 1832. He excelled in his studies at West Point, although he himself said he spent too much time at athletics and outdoor activities. He was among the top three students in French and mathematics, and did well in history. Meigs graduated fifth out of a class of forty-nine in 1836 and had more good-conduct merits than two thirds of his classmates.

Meigs received a commission as a second lieutenant in the 1st U.S. Artillery, but most of his army service was with the Corps of Engineers, in which he worked on important engineering projects and proved to be adroit at mapping. He also served under the command of then Lieutenant Robert E. Lee to make navigational improvements on the Mississippi River.

In August 1837, Meigs and Lee traveled together by steamer from Pittsburgh to St. Louis. They were tasked with removing the small islands formed by the Mississippi River near the banks of St. Louis, which threatened water traffic and the growth of the city. St. Louis had grown steadily in recent years; the population was 5,600 when Missouri was admitted into the Union in 1821, but by 1840 it would be three times as large. Lee himself recorded more than five hundred homes were built and more than 162 steamboats used the ports there in the twelve months after they finished their work.

Meigs had said that he had remembered Lee

with pleasure and affection in "his intimate associations with Lieutenant Lee, then a man in the vigor of youthful strength, with a noble and commanding presence, and an admirable, graceful, and athletic figure. He was one with whom nobody ever wished or ventured to take a liberty, though kind and generous to his subordinates, admired by all women, and respected by all men. He was the model of a soldier and the beau ideal of a Christian Man."

Lee was slow and methodical in his work. The local citizenry was impatient with his doggedness and his imperviousness to their harangues, but he moved at his own pace. Lee and Meigs were adamant that the port of St. Louis not get cut off from deep water.

According to Dowdey, Lee "went out with the civilian workers every morning about sunrise and worked beside them during the heat of the day. A steamboat moored to the bank was used as headquarters, and there the patrician lieutenant (as some of the townspeople had found him) shared the men's rations and sometimes ate at the same table in the cabin—though an observer pointed out that he never became familiar."

Lee "maintained and preserved under all circumstances his dignity and gentlemanly bearing, winning, and commanding esteem, regard, and respect of every man under him," recalled Mayor John F. Darby.

Meigs amused himself by hunting, fishing, and painting while in St. Louis, but his letters to his family were filled with homesickness and an aversion to his hotel room. He complained of walls with peeling plaster that had a dirty smell, which he attempted to cover up with cologne he'd brought along on the trip.

Lee and Meigs were successful in diverting the river and St. Louis grew remarkably afterwards, with the knowledge that their deep-water port would allow for commerce and shipping. Lee and Meigs only worked with each other that one summer. But a friendship had been formed.

Through the efforts of Lee and Meigs,
St. Louis's port was made a safer harbor,
and was allowed to grow. By 1850-1860
St. Louis was a major metropolitan area.

Robert E. Lee, the nation's ablest soldier, in his Confederate uniform, which he donned after Virginia seceded from the Union.

CHAPTER 4
ROBERT E. LEE
SAVES ARLINGTON

Robert E. Lee rode up the winding lane that led to the mansion on horseback. He was returning once again, this time from Texas, to Arlington. When he had come home from the

Mexican War, an admiring throng had greeted him in front of the massive pillars of Arlington. But this time he dismounted alone. Without realizing it yet, an immense responsibility awaited him.

The Custis family estate had by this time become home to Robert and Mary Lee, and Robert and Mary spent a great deal of their married life traveling between U.S. Army duty stations and Arlington. Six of the seven Lee children were born at Arlington.

Robert and Mary Lee's bedroom at Arlington.

By age fifty Robert E. Lee had traveled the country with the Army Corps of Engineers, and had served bravely and gallantly in the Mexican War. He had proven himself to be the great soldier many people believed he could be. Talented and slightly reckless, his feats of daring and cunning proved invaluable to the U.S. Army's advance into Mexico. And he had made himself indispensable to one of the two great commanders of the campaign, General Winfield Scott, and was handsomely rewarded for his successes.

But in 1857 Robert had other pressing matters. He had a large family, and Mary was sick. She suffered from rheumatoid arthritis, a debilitating disease for which there was no medicine. Visits to hot springs were the only known way to relieve pain, but not cure the ailment. By now, Mary had a home with three spirited sons and four daughters, and her father's health was failing rapidly. She was at her wits' end and complained to Robert via letter. "I will do my best," she wrote to Lee, "but you can do much better . . . it is time now that you were with your family."

Mary Custis Lee and son Robert E. Lee, Jr.

"In the 1850s, when communications and travel were so slow, it was understood that for an officer of Lee's rank and social class a death in the family required time off, and he had no difficulty in obtaining two months' leave," wrote biographer Michael Korda. "I can see that I have at last to decide the question, which I have staved off for 20 years," Lee wrote his friend, fellow officer Albert Sydney Johnston. "Whether I am to continue in the Army all my life or to leave it . . . My preferences which have clung to me from boyhood impel me to adopt the former course, but yet I feel that a man's has claims too."

In October of that year George Washington Custis died of pneumonia at the age of seventy-six. Mary was grief-stricken. Her mother, Mary Lee Fitzhugh Custis, had passed away in 1853, and now, with the death of her father, she felt quite alone.

In his last few days, Custis had professed to his daughter that he had regretted not turning toward God in the way that his wife and daughter had. "God have mercy on me in my last moments," he told Mary, "I am so glad I have a pious family. Lay me beside my blessed wife."

"In contrast to his wife's quiet, private funeral service, G.W.P. Custis's was a great public affair. On a bright autumn day, six slaves carried the mahogany coffin from the drawing room of the mansion to the gravesite next to Mrs. Custis's," wrote historian John Perry. "Newspapers throughout the country carried Mr. Custis's obituary. *The National Intelligencer* echoed the sentiments of many: Thousands from this country and from foreign lands who have visited Arlington to commune with our departed friend . . . will not forget the charm thrown over all by the ease, grace, interest, and vivacity of the manners and conversation of him whose voice, alas!, is now silent."

Suddenly responsible for the complex series of estates and farms that her father had overseen his entire life, Mary was completely overwhelmed. "Along with everyone else who knew him well, Mary had long recognized that her father 'was not very methodical in the management of his affairs.' A clearer picture of just how unmethodical he was emerged after Robert arrived at Arlington and Custis's will was unsealed."

"Balding and undistinguished in appearance, with some wan pretensions to learning, Martha Washington's fifty-year-old grandson was a garrulous dilettante. He indifferently administered his inherited properties, [and] was slovenly in his housekeeping and his personal habits. . . ." wrote Clifford Dowdey.

The Lee family, and Robert in particular, was at a crossroads. Custis's estate was insolvent. Mary and Robert had been left Arlington to live in until such time their eldest son could take possession. It was now Robert's job to return the estate to a satisfactory situation and keep the house in the family. His own family's wealth had fallen out of their hands after his eldest brother had squandered it in a well-publicized scandal. So Robert felt an enormous responsibility to his family and their posterity.

"The family's problems nearly overwhelmed Lee the moment he arrived back at Arlington on November 11. His first shock was the extent to which Mary Custis Lee had become an invalid—nothing in her letters had prepared Lee for the pain she was in, or for the fact that at the age of forty-nine she could hardly even move around the house without assistance," wrote Korda.

"I almost dread his seeing my crippled state," she had written a friend before Robert's return.

Robert was named the executor of Custis's will. Robert and Mary had inherited the stewardship of three estates, several scattered land holdings in the Chesapeake region, and 196 slaves. Many of the farms were producing little to no cash crops. Mills and slave quarters needed repairs. The boundaries to several of these holdings were ambiguous, and Lee estimated that the entire estate, all totaled, was in arrears of $10,000, and a hefty mortgage placed on Arlington itself totaled $50,000. All huge sums in those days.

"He has left me an unpleasant legacy," Lee wrote. He arrived to find that "everything is in ruins and will have to be rebuilt." Lee wrote to his eldest son, "I can now see little prospect of fulfilling the provisions of your grandfather's will within the space of five years, within which he expected it to be accomplished and his people liberated," wrote Lee referring to the estate's slaves.

Virginia state law maintained any freed slaves would have to move out of Virginia, and that the remaining family would be responsible for their welfare and maintenance. Custis had set aside no allowance for the freedmen in his will. Even Mary lamented, "There is no such provision nor indeed any for their maintenance which proceeded from his usual want of care in matters of business and I presume a belief that we should take care of them."

This caused an immediate and lingering problem for the Lees and the estate. "Lee had interpreted the Custis will to mean that all bequests must be paid out before manumission. The will itself actually called for land to be sold to pay the debts and legacies, and never states that these obligations should take precedence over freeing the slaves. Soon after he arrived at Arlington, Lee petitioned the courts to give him a ruling over the competing demands of the Custis will," wrote Elizabeth Brown Pryor. Lee petitioned that "the emancipation of the slaves should be postponed till said legacies are raised, and the debts of the estate are paid off."

The slaves, knowing that their freedom awaited them, were not happy to find that Lee had set the estate's solvency above their own desires and rights. By all means, he improved their working conditions. But the estate had grown sloppy in Custis's last year, and the farms had gone to seed in many cases. The field hands had performed little work in recent years and were resentful of being put to work. Getting the slaves to put forth effort was difficult. In some cases, slaves had to be rented out, which understandably infuriated them even more. But Lee could figure out no other course.

"Lee went at the complex problem in the only way he knew how to work: with a master plan, he gave finite attention to each of a multitude of details, one detail at a time, proceeding one day at a time. Never considering any quick way, any spectacular stroke, at the age of fifty he became a planter," wrote biographer Dowdey. "In doing this Lee showed that, with all his gentleness of nature, he was not a soft man. While his sense of honor required him to fulfill the letter of Custis's will with scrupulous exactitude, nothing required him to follow his father-in-law's sentimental indulgence of field workers. To Lee they were the same as any troops under his command."

But Lee led his enslaved "troops" with a marked ambivalence. "However difficult it might be to deal with the numerous problems of the Custis estate, nothing caused Lee more suffering or singed his reputation as much as his father-in-law's slaves," wrote Michael Korda. "Lee was never an enthusiast of slavery, and his experience with the Custis slaves further soured him on the institution."

Despite these difficulties, Lee concentrated on returning the estate to solvency. He and Mary also continued with a plan to educate the slaves under their care until they were officially freed on December 29, 1862, at which time most were already behind Union lines, at the federally held Arlington.

Up to the time of the war, Lee worked very hard at righting the estate's waning fortunes, and staved off economic disaster for his family and generations to come.

In the meantime, the life of the Lee family took on a more pleasant dynamic. Mary Lee was happy to have her husband back at home, as were their children. There was a certain serenity in returning to a more normal family life.

A guest at Arlington observed Lee's face in quiet repose as he read to his family assembled about the table one night. She thought to herself: "You certainly look more like a great man than any one I have ever seen."

Mrs. Lee and her mother had made an

equally favorable impression on a lady who visited Arlington in the spring of 1849. "We had tea in the Washington teacups, and Mrs. Lee took me into the tangled neglected gardens, full of rose-buds, and allowed me to pick my fill of the sweet dainty Bon Silene variety, which she told me blossomed all winter. What a view that was! . . . Mrs. Lee had the face of a genius: a wealth of dark hair, carelessly put up, gave her fine head the air of one of Romney's portraits."

According to the historians at Arlington House, "The flower garden was as important to the Lee family as any room in the main house. It was here they came to entertain, study, seek solitude, pray, admire the beauties of nature, work the soil, read, play, and even bury their pets. The garden was well known among their friends and relatives, and plants from Arlington's garden and the conservatory found their way into many other Virginia gardens. When he was at home, it was Colonel Lee's custom to gather rosebuds in the garden each morning and place one beside the plate of each of his daughters, the youngest getting the smallest bud, and so on up to the eldest."

Lee once wrote to a friend, "The Country looks very sweet now, and the hill at Arlington covered with verdure, and perfumed by the blossoms of the trees, the flowers of the Garden. Honey-Suckles, yellow Jasmine, &c. is more to my taste than at any other season of the year. But the brightest flower there blooming is my daughter . . . [I] hurry home to her every day."

"[We] found your grandfather at the Washington depot, Daniel and the old carriage and horses, and young Daniel on the colt Mildred. Your mother, grandfather, Mary Eliza, the little people, and the baggage, I thought load enough for the carriage, so Rooney and I took our feet in our hands and walked over. . . . The snow impeded the carriage as well as us, and we reached here shortly after it," Robert E. Lee would write later to his son at West Point in 1851, describing a typical Christmas at Arlington. "The children were delighted at getting back, and passed the evening in devising pleasure for the morrow. They were in upon us before day on Christmas morning, to overhaul their stockings. . . . I need not describe to you our amusements, you have witnessed them so often; nor the turkey, cold ham, plum-pudding, mince pies, etc., at dinner." "Rooney" was the Lee's second boy, William Henry Fitzhugh.

Even years later, in June of 1860 Robert E. Lee would write to his daughter Annie, "I was very glad to receive, my Sweet Annie, your letter . . . to hear that the garden, trees, and hill at Arlington looked beautiful."

The importance of those gardens never faded in the family's memory.

A rose grown in the gardens at Arlington National Cemetery.

Montgomery C. Meigs at the height of his powers. The supplier of the Union Army and the builder of the Capitol dome.

CHAPTER 5

MEIGS AND THE GREAT DOME

Montgomery C. Meigs had had it. By 1858 Meigs and Thomas U. Walter, the architect of the Capitol building, had been at each other for some time now. Two massive egos clashed at every possible opportunity. Neither would give the other an inch.

In 1853, the War Department had assumed control of the Capitol extension project. Then Secretary of War, Jefferson Davis, appointed thirty-six-year-old Meigs to run the project. He took the reins of the project energetically, immersing himself in the study of architecture, acoustics, heating, ventilation, and decorating. The primary goal of the project was to provide well-ventilated chambers where the nation's legislators could hear and speak with ease.

While the dome and Capitol extension were designed by architect Thomas U. Walter, the construction, funding, and logistical challenges were Meigs's responsibility. One significant engineering feat he accomplished was how to raise the cast iron to build the dome. Meigs designed a scaffold that rose from within the center of the Capitol Rotunda with a triangular footprint to stand clear of the floor's unsupported center. He added a mast and a boom, each eighty feet long, to the top of the scaffold to lift the ironwork into place. A steam engine housed in a shack on the roof provided enough power to lift twenty thousand pounds of material. To fuel the steam engine, he first used the wood from the old smaller dome, which had been removed.

However, Meigs and Walter were a classic clash of egos. Both had powerful allies in government, and fought to a stand off. The two argued at every turn, and could agree on nothing.

Meigs criticized Walter's designs and opinions, and Walter could not abide Meigs's merest suggestions on how to execute those designs. At one point, the Secretary of War proposed to create a board to oversee the plans submitted by Walters before they were handed over to Meigs.

"I found upon my table tonight a card from Colonel Robert E. Lee of the cavalry. He asks to see me at the War Department tomorrow at 10 a.m.," Meigs recorded in his diary.

"John Lee called and told me that Robert E. Lee had been sent for by the Secretary and told him that he was in trouble about the dispute between me and Mr. Walter; that he was determined not to dismiss Walter," Meigs continued. "Lee told him he did not see how such a board could work and that he did not desire to be upon it. The Secretary named Lee and Humphreys, Captain of Topogs [Topography]. Did not know whom else to select.

"John Lee told Robert Lee something of the matter in dispute and advised him to keep clear of such a board. Robert Lee came to see me, having told the Secretary he must see me before he could answer about the matter."

In the next day's entry, Meigs reported, "I saw Robert Lee today. He said that I ought to manage matters as to get along with the Secretary, etc. I asked him to come to my house to hear a part of the correspondence in the case which I had,

*The home of Montgomery C. Meigs
still stands today.*

arising between Mr. Walter and myself, and then to judge whether I had not been patient and prudent.

"He did not like to take up the time and thought that this was foreign to the matter which the secretary had put upon him. He said that he should not accept the place if he could help it. He was a lieutenant colonel of Cavalry and now if on duty would have command of his regiment, and that is his proper place, as soon as he could get through his private business and return to duty, was at the head of his regiment," scribbled Meigs. "He said that he did not think the Secretary had a clear idea of what he intended this board to do."

Meigs read the letters to Lee. According to Meigs's journal Lee advised him, "If I was in

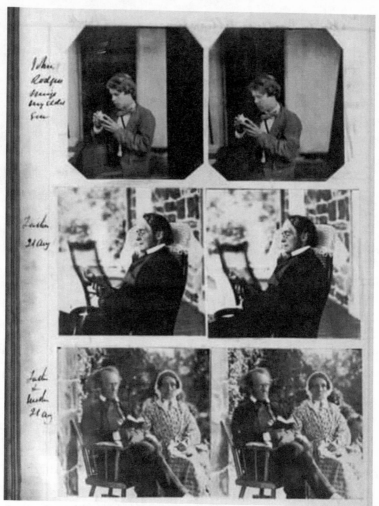

A page of the Montgomery C. Meigs family photo album. A young John Rodgers Meigs is at the top of the page.

charge, Mr. Walter should obey me. After this he left, but he still advised that I should not be troublesome or obstinate, etc. I saw, however, that he thought I was right in my position."

Meigs and Walter endured each other throughout the building of the project and the completion of the dome. He was always grateful for Lee's help in the matter.

While Lee attempted to deal with the burden of his father-in-law's estate, events regarding the slavery question had begun to flare up around the country. Bleeding Kansas had long been a source of sad news, where abolitionists clashed in bloody conflict with supporters of slavery. Now another such event happened much nearer to Washington, pulling Robert away from home once again.

On October 17, 1859, Brevet Colonel Robert E. Lee was requested to lead a detachment of U.S. marines on a raid to recapture the arsenal Harpers Ferry, which had been taken by force by abolitionist John Brown and a small band of followers (including his own sons) the day before. Lee led the raid in his civilian clothes, as he had been on personal leave he did not have a uniform with him. President James Buchannan and War Department Secretary Floyd spoke with Lee in person. Lieutenant J.E.B. Stuart accompanied Lee on the train ride to Harpers Ferry on the Baltimore and Ohio (B&O) Railroad and offered himself as Lee's aide-de-camp. Brown's men held a building for two days while the troops were mobilized. On October 18, Stuart approached Brown's men under a white flag and offered them a peaceful arrest, but they rejected the offer. Within minutes of their rejection, the buildings were stormed and the raid on Harpers Ferry came to a quick and bloody end.

Four months later Lee resumed his military life as a cavalry officer.

Lincoln's inauguration took place under the shadows of the unfinished dome. Lincoln insisted on its completion during the course of the war. Meigs oversaw the construction of the Capitol Building's dome throughout the course of the war.

General Winfield Scott, one of the biggest heroes of the Mexican War, was an old man by the time the Civil War commenced. His confidence in Lee, his protégé, was unshakable.

CHAPTER 6
FLEEING ARLINGTON

Robert E. Lee was pacing the floors of Arlington. He had a momentous decision to make. With Washington glittering below the front windows of the great mansion, Lee mulled over his decision.

He had spent a very long interview with his mentor General Winfield Scott, who discussed with him the offer of heading the Union Army. Francis P. Blair, a consummate Washington insider and confidant of President Lincoln, had met with Lee previously to make the offer on behalf of the president.

His daughter Mary Custis Lee recalled, "It was on Sunday, the 14th of April 1861, that, coming out of the old Christ Church No. Alexandria. We were greeted with the intelligence, of the fall of 'Sumter.' The excitement and confusion were intense and every one flocked around Papa, following him in a crowd of ladies as well as gentlemen to the door of my Aunt's, Mrs. Fitzhugh, where we habitually stopped after church—He was perfectly calm, though evidently much moved and I remember his saying 'poor General Anderson! He was a determined man, and I know held out to the last.'

"On Thursday, the 18th, He drove over to Washington, not returning till late in the evening. That was his final interview with Gen. Scott; Cameron, Secretary of War, & Seward, both being present and, as I understand afterwards, every inducement being held out to persuade him to accept command of the Federal Army," Mary continued.

"I remember him saying to me subsequently, 'I told Mr. Seward that if he could give me the whole four millions of slaves into my own hands tomorrow, they would not weigh one moment in the balance against the Union. That I was not contending for the perpetuation of slavery'—or words to that effect. When he returned after dark, evidently worn and harassed, I told him that we had had a visit that was from a cousin of ours, just from 'Richmond' & though he had left the (day before) morning of the passage of the ordinance of Secession—he was convinced that it would pass very soon, and had been extremely anxious to see him (Papa)."

She continued, "He several times said 'I wish I could have seen him,' & plied me with many more questions than I could answer as to exactly what he had said; adding, 'I presume the poor old State will go out. I don't think she need do so, yet at least, but so many are trying to push her out that she will have to go I suppose.'"

Lee spent all night replaying the conversations with Blair and Scott in his head.

He had told Blair that, ". . . though opposed to secession and deprecating war, I could take no part in an invasion of the Southern States."

And Scott's angry proclamation had been ringing in his ears: "Lee, you have made the greatest mistake of your life. But I feared it would be so." Lee had suggested that he could sit the war out, rather than serve, to which Scott rebutted, "No one should remain in government without being actively employed!"

The next morning he sent the following letter to Scott.

Winfield Scott
Arlington, Washington City P.O.,
April 20, 1861
General:

Since my interview with you on the 18th instant I have felt that I ought not longer to retain my commission in the Army. I therefore tender my resignation, which I request you will recommend for acceptance.

It would have been presented at once, but for the struggle it has cost me to separate myself from a service to which I have devoted all the best years of my life & all the ability I possessed.

During the whole of that time, more than 30 years, I have experienced nothing but kindness from my superiors, & the most cordial friendship from my companions. To no one Genl have I been as much indebted as to yourself for uniform kindness & consideration, & it has always been my ardent desire to merit your approbation.

I shall carry with me to the grave the most grateful recollections of your kind consideration, & your name & fame will always be dear to me. Save in the defence of my native State, I never desire again to draw my sword.

Be pleased to accept my most earnest wishes for the continuance of your happiness & prosperity & believe me most truly yours

R. E. Lee

"He read from the rough draft," wrote Lee's daughter Mary Custis Lee, "saying, when he had finished, 'This is a copy of the letter which I have sent to Gen. Scott. I wrote it early this morning when I first came down and dispatched Perry over to Washington with it before breakfast,' adding, 'I mention this to you to show you that I have not at all been influenced by the exciting news from Baltimore [i.e., the riots].' None of us could speak for several moments. He presently said, 'I suppose you all think I have done very wrong.'

"That same afternoon, a cousin (poor Orton Williams) who was on Gen Scott's staff, and a great favorite of his, rode over, and first mentioned the subject to which had been engrossing our thoughts all day, adding that 'now that "Cousin Robert" had resigned everyone seemed to be doing so,'" continued the general's daughter. "He also told us how heavily the blow had fallen upon the 'poor old General,' as he called him, how very unwell, and lying upon a sofa, he had refused to see every one, and mourned as for the loss of a son. To some one, Gen. Cullum, I think, who rather lightly alluded to the fact, he said, with great emotion, 'Don't mention Robert Lee's name to me again, I cannot bear it!' And Papa, that same day, said to me in response to a question I had asked about Gen. Scott—'Yes, he is going to hold on to the Union,—but I believe it will kill him; I don't think he can live through it all.'

"The Secession of Virginia was known now, and Papa was followed by the crowd, and button-holed in the street, as if their faith was pinned on him alone. A rumor had prevailed there that he had been arrested as soon as he resigned, and great was the emotion expressed at seeing him safe and well," continued Mary. "Papa said quietly, 'You see how unfortunate it is to yield to excitement, let me beg of you all, whatever happens, and there are probably very trying times before you, when I may not be with you to advise you, that you will listen to your reason, not to your impulses. Try and keep cool in all circumstances.'"

"My husband has wept tears of blood over this terrible war, but as a man of honor and as a Virginian, he must follow the destiny of his State," wrote Mary Custis Lee to a friend. She then wrote to her daughter, Mildred, away at school, "With a sad and heavy heart, my dear child, I write, for the prospects before us are sad indeed, and as I think both parties are wrong in this fratricidal war there is nothing comforting even in the hope that God may prosper the right, for I see no right in the matter."

Two days after tendering his resignation to Scott, Robert E. Lee found himself in Richmond, Virginia, already at work. He was among the first five generals named in the Confederate army. The northern press skewered Lee, and one paper went so far as to name him as this century's Benedict Arnold.

"About the same time, she had a revealing firsthand look at the government's efforts to turn public opinion against her husband and to justify confiscating her property," wrote John Perry.

Mary was in town on the same day the New York 7th Regiment arrived in Washington. "As I was going out of town, one of the members of the regiment who I had known at West Point came to the door of my carriage to greet me," recalled Mary.

"What are you doing here in this guise?" she asked him.

"We were summoned here to defend the Capitol which we were told was in imminent danger and expected to see Jeff Davis with an army of at least 30,000 men on the Arlington Heights," the young man responded.

"Come over and judge for yourself. I will secure you against capture," Mary replied.

However, the dark clouds over the mansion continued to gather. With Lee's resignation, Arlington was transformed from the celebrated estate of a legendary family to the home of a traitor. It no longer served as a proud reminder of the country's past; it was now tarnished by a man who had not only refused to lead the nation's army against armed rebellion, but would discard his oath to his country and draw his sword against the Union. The giant edifice was a daily reminder to Washingtonians of the day that the South had withdrawn, taking many of its top soldiers with it. For the next five to ten years it would be at the center of sadness, anguish, and would serve as a symbol to the nation of its own impending and seemingly impossible demise.

Arlington was precariously placed. In a military situation, the Arlington Heights looked over the city, and a solid battery of artillery could make short work of the city from that vantage point, easily striking the Capitol Building and the White House. Both armies knew it. But no one knew it more than Robert E. Lee.

"I am very anxious about you," he wrote Mary on April 26. "You have to move and go to some point of safety, which you must select. The Mount Vernon plate and pictures ought to be secured. Keep quiet while you remain and in your preparation. War is inevitable, and there is no telling when it will burst around you. Virginia, yesterday, joined the Confederate states. What policy they may adopt I cannot conjecture. May God bless and preserve you, and have mercy on all our people."

He wrote her again on April 30, "You had better prepare all things for removal, that is, the plate, pictures, etc. and be prepared at any moment." He wrote her three days later, "I want you to be in a place of safety."

But Mary was stubborn in her refusal to leave Arlington—until a visitor came calling.

Mary's aunt Martha Custis Peter's grandson, Orton Williams, came to the house. Secretly dispatched by General Winfield Scott, he arrived dressed in his Union Army uniform. The twenty-two-year-old man waited on the portico, but after a while he could take it no longer, and bounded up the stairs of the mansion into the living quarters.

"You've got to get out now. Union troops are ready to take Arlington Heights," he said, warning her that they would storm the house within days. Mary was spurred to action. She started making arrangements, though she made no move to actually leave. Orton came back too the next day to tell her the attack had been delayed, but that it was definitely still coming. Orton resigned his commission the next day, and took a new commission in the Confederate Army.

"Beginning her preparations at last, Mary

moved quickly to safeguard as many belongings as possible. The family silver, Washington's personal papers, and Custis and Lee family papers were packed in two crates and sent by rail to Robert in Richmond. Books and engravings were locked away in closets. Carpets and drapes— including a set of damask draperies from Martha Washington—went into the attic. The famous punch bowl with its ship painted on the bottom, the Washington state china, and the other Mount Vernon relics were securely crated and locked in the cellar," wrote Perry.

By May 8, paintings, wine, food, clothes, housekeeping supplies, and the Arlington piano were loaded into a wagon, and Mary sent her daughter Agnes to Ravenswood and her aunt Maria Fitzhugh's home for safety's sake. Mary stayed behind.

Oddly, Mary focused on the gardens. "The spring weather had been unusually chilly and wet, and the flower gardens had started the season far behind schedule. On April 10, Mary had written Mildred that it was still too dark and cold for most of the flowers," reported Perry.

"We have had some lovely callas in the greenhouse and those parma violets, but there is so little sun for things to bloom," she had written. But here, a month later, the gardens exploded in a profusion of green and now gorgeous colors began bursting forth.

Mary wrote to Robert on May 9, as she lingered at Arlington to the last, "I never saw the country-side more beautiful, perfectly radiant. The yellow jasmine is in full bloom and perfuming the air, but a deathlike stillness prevails every-where. You hear no sound from Washington, not a soul moving about. We may well exclaim 'Can such things be? Can man trample upon all his Creator has lavished upon him of love and beauty?' I think the hours and years must be commencing when Satan is to be let loose upon the earth . . . and while we must feel that our sins both personal and national merit the chastise-ment of the Almighty, we may still implore Him to pare us and with mercy not in wrath to visit us."

Robert replied from the headquarters in Richmond, "I am glad to hear you are at peace, and enjoying the sweet weather and beautiful flowers. You had better complete your arrange-ments and retire further from the scene of war. It may burst upon you at any time. It is sad to think of the devastation, if not ruin, it may bring upon a spot so endeared to us. But God's will be done. We must be resigned."

"I would have greatly preferred remaining at home & having my children around me," she wrote to one of her daughters, "but as it would greatly increase your Father's anxiety I shall go." She made an eerily accurate prediction: "I fear that this will be the scene of conflict &

my beautiful home endeared by a thousand associations may become a field of carnage."

Suddenly signs were everywhere that something was going on. Washington had come to life, and the river was cluttered with boats and tugs and barges and all manner of vessel. Mary knew what was coming. The family pets were left with the domestic staff, and the keys of the mansion she turned over to her most trusted servant, Selina Grey.

"And on a beautiful morning in the idle of May, 1861, Mary Custis Lee took one last walk—slowly and stiffly, leaning on her crutches—through the garden her parents had laid out more than half a century before, now awash in colors and fragrances of spring. Here was her mother's favorite spot. And here were little plots where each of the girls had planted whatever pleased them. Mildred's was smaller than the rest because she used part of her space to bury her cats in when they died. Mary stooped slowly, stiffly, and cut a moss rose from the arbor," wrote Perry.

Mary climbed with difficulty into the carriage, leaning heavily on her son Custis. As she looked back toward the house, she could see through her own voluminous tears that the servants too were crying. The carriage lurched forward, just beginning the ride to Ravenswood. Arlington slowly disappeared behind the rolling hills.

"She looked down at the freshly cut rose in

her lap: a rose of Arlington. She wondered if she would ever see another one," Perry wrote.

Little more than a week later, under cover of moonlight, ten thousand troops quietly crossed the Potomac and took control of Arlington Heights and Arlington House. The mansion was now under control of Federal troops.

Mary would never again spend the night at Arlington.

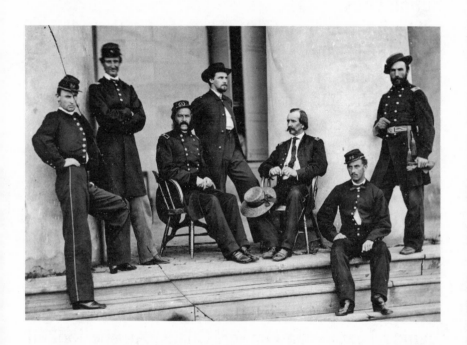

Brig. Gen. Gustavus A. DeRussey (third from left) and staff on portico of Arlington House. Throughout the war, Union officers and soldiers were consistently photographed on the Arlington grounds. It remained a celebrated place, despite its complex history.

Secretary of War Edwin C. Stanton remained a staunch foe of all those who had left the Union Army to join the Southern cause.

CHAPTER 7
ARLINGTON GONE

On March 9, 1864, Abraham Lincoln appointed Ulysses S. Grant commander-in-chief of all Union armies. That spring, Grant launched several military campaigns that he had hoped would end the war. Two large attacks opened the spring campaign. The Red River campaign had begun in March, in Louisiana. It was another Union disaster, plagued by miscommunications and poor planning, as thirty thousand Union troops continually faltered against fifteen thousand Confederates. But the real prizefight began in May of that year, when Grant himself took to the field and launched a series of bloody attacks against Lee. The Battle of the Wilderness, Spotsylvania, North Anna River, and Cold Harbor were a series of brutal battles in May and June. Grant seemingly lost each engagement but continued to re-engage Lee at the next opportunity. Lee's losses in men in each battle were proportionately greater, thus reducing the overall size of his army. It was a slow, ugly whittling down of the Confederate army in which tens of thousands were sacrificed.

As the conflict escalated the hospitals in Washington were flooded with the wounded and dying. To call these hospitals was in many cases a misnomer, as many were converted churches, public halls, or governmental buildings.

"Maimed and wounded . . . arrived by hundreds as long as the waves of sorrow came streaming back from the fields of slaughter . . . They came groping, hobbling, and faltering, so faint and so longing for rest that one's heart bled at the piteous sight," wrote Washington journalist Noah Brooks.

The city's cemeteries were filled to bursting,

and the National Cemetery was also filled to capacity. In order to relieve some of the pressure, it was agreed that the U.S. Army would begin interring soldiers along the northern border of the Arlington estate. The spot chosen was approximately a half mile from the mansion itself.

The burials at Arlington began one month before it officially became a national cemetery. The first person to be buried there was Private William Christman of the 67th Pennsylvania Infantry, on May 13, 1864. Christman had died at age twenty-one from complications due to measles at Washington's Lincoln General Hospital. He had been a farmer, newly recruited, and had never even seen battle. His grave marker was a simple pine board, painted white with his name lettered on it in black.

According to Arlington historian Robert M. Poole, "The private's grave was situated in a poorly drained sector of Arlington down among the low hills skirting what was then the Alexandria-Georgetown Pike. This far corner of the estate was out of sight of the mansion, where Union officers lived and worked. Not wishing to have the view marred by new graves, they directed the first burials well away from the house."

Christman was joined by Private William H. McKinney, cavalryman, Pennsylvania, who was buried later that same day. A day later Private William Blatt, 19th Regiment, Pennsylvania

Infantry, was also interred after dying from injuries sustained in the Wilderness Campaign.

Six more followed quickly, from various parts of the country, including soldiers from New York, Vermont, Maine, New Jersey, Massachusetts, and North Carolina (this last one being a Confederate soldier).

According to Poole, the burials at Arlington were originally "an act of improvisation born of necessity to process the war's carnage before it became a public health or public relations nuisance." But for the Union army, the transformation of Robert E. Lee's plantation home into a national cemetery was a symbolic victory as well as a practical decision. Indeed, as Poole writes, "More than a touch of vengeance was involved."

The driving force behind this decision was none other than Montgomery C. Meigs, Lee's former comrade-in-arms.

In the fall of 1860, as a result of a disagreement over procurement contracts, Montgomery Meigs had "incurred the ill will" of the secretary of war, John B. Floyd, and was "banished to Tortugas in the Gulf of Mexico to construct fortifications at that place and at Key West." But upon the resignation of Floyd a few months later, Meigs was recalled to his work on the aqueduct at Washington. By the time the war started, Meigs was the quartermaster of the Union Army.

As historian Robert Poole pointed out, "Former Army comrades who had admired Lee now turned against him. None was more outspoken than Montgomery C. Meigs, a fellow West Point graduate who had served under Lee in the engineer corps but who now considered him a traitor who deserved hanging."

In regard to Lee, Joseph Johnston, and Jefferson Davis, all of whom he had known, Meigs wrote, "No man who ever took the oath to support the Constitution as an officer of our army or navy, a Graduate of West Point, a member of Congress or the cabinet, and who has since actively engaged in rebellion in any civil or military station should escape without loss of all his goods and civil rights and expatriation. The leaders should be put formally out of the way, if possible, by sentence of death, executed if ever caught."

Speaking of his zeal for the Union and its cause, Meigs's wife wrote to her mother, saying that Montgomery's "soul seems to be on fire with indignation at the reason of those wicked men who have laid the deep plot to overthrow our government and destroy the most noble fabric of free the world has ever seen . . . He looks so dreadfully stern when he talks of the rebellion that I do not like to look at him but he does not look more stern and relentless than he feels."

Meigs himself wrote of it, as "a great and holy war. God is with us. Who shall be against us."

Meigs noted that the war would "hasten by a few years the deaths of certain thousands of men, the mourning of widows and orphans. All must die, all must mourn in time."

Given his close relationships especially to Lee and Davis, this was a rather radical response.

Meigs had been defended by none other than Senator Jefferson Davis when he was in the midst of his difficulties with former Secretary of War Floyd. Floyd, an unscrupulous man, did not like that Meigs was fair and honest about granting contracts, and wanted Floyd to favor certain businessmen. Meigs had refused, and Davis supported him. When bridges didn't make it in time to Ambrose Burnside who was on the banks of the Rappahannock, Meigs came under fire.

"Meigs responded that he had sent them out in a timely manner but that field commanders along the way had been responsible for their delay," wrote Steve Rolfe in an article about Meigs. "This kind of seemingly constant squabbling began to get Meigs somewhat depressed by early 1863, and it didn't help when a few Senators began to question his loyalty because of his pre-war close friendship with Jefferson Davis. Was this the reason, some thought, that supplies were allegedly slow in arriving? Was this the reason why the pontoons were supposedly late? Fortunately, Meigs had more supporters than detractors. When Senator James Lane of Kansas accused Meigs of disloyalty on the Senate floor in late January, Senator Henry Wilson of Massachusetts came to the Quartermaster General's defense and told Lane that Meigs was as loyal as Lane:

A question has been raised here about the loyalty of General Meigs, and why? It is said that he was Jeff Davis' friend, and Jeff Davis was his patron. I do not think there is anything in that. Jefferson Davis stood by General Meigs when John B. Floyd undertook to crush him. Floyd was not only a traitor but a thief, and left the government only when there seemed nothing more for him to steal. Davis was not a thief, but a traitor to the country. I do not think any of us ever accused Jeff Davis of being connected dishonorably with money affairs, or, in the ordinary matters of legislation, to be a corrupt man; but we knew that Floyd was partial and corrupt. In the controversy that General Meigs had with Floyd, he was sustained by Jefferson Davis. He was also sustained by nearly all of us on this side of the Chamber. As to the loyalty of General Meigs, I do not think there is a man in America who has a right to question it.

In fact, Meigs was known to be of the utmost character. He had been recommended for the job of quartermaster by famed Washington insider and power broker Francis Blair, founder of the Republican Party, who wrote of Meigs that he had "energy, industry, knowledge of other wants of the army—his zeal in the cause our army is about to vindicate—above all his well-known probity, punctuality, and string common sense in dealing with men, fit his for his service."

Despite his many connections to these men with whom he had served—or perhaps because of it —Meigs held firm that they deserved the ultimate punishment for their treason. As the war went on, many more people agreed with him.

At the end of the war Meigs wanted "Congress [to] pass a law banishing [the rebel] leaders if by military [action] or by Presidential pardon or clemency they escape immediate punishment."

Meigs's biographer David W. Miller wrote, "Meigs' reconstruction attitude was against 'compromise or soft measure with traitors and murders of loyal people and institutions' . . . Disgust was directed to West Point graduates who had taken the oath to defend the constitution . . . we're given public education, and when the enemy arose 'hasten to join' him."

In Secretary of War Edwin M. Stanton, Meigs found a temperamental but kindred spirit.

A native of Steubenville, Ohio, Stanton ran a

successful law practice before President James Buchanan appointed him attorney general in 1860. Stanton was known for being an outspoken abolitionist with a quick temper.

"Stanton, a Washington lawyer from the Midwest, was a bitter, treacherous man, driven by choleric energy and appetite for power. Though a democrat and a slippery politician, he was among the men whose aggressions found release in the hostile aspects of abolitionism, and he acted with the Radicals in the bonds of common hatred of the South," wrote Civil War historian Clifford Dowdey.

Stanton had written the former president, "The dreadful disaster of Sunday [Battle of Bull Run] can scarcely be mentioned. The imbecility of this administration has culminated in that catastrophe, and irretrievable misfortune and national disgrace are to be added to the ruin of all peaceful pursuits and national bankruptcy as the result of Lincoln's 'running the machine' for five months."

Stanton was known to completely ignore the requests of Lincoln, and sometimes acted in concert with other cabinet officials, including Salmon Chase, behind the president's back. Lincoln was well aware of Stanton's arrogance and duplicity.

William H. Crook, one of Lincoln's bodyguards, related a wonderful story about Stanton's explosive personality and Lincoln's handling of him.

The two men were often at variance when it came to matters of discipline in the army. On one occasion, I have heard, Secretary Stanton was particularly angry with one of the generals. He was eloquent about him. 'I would like to tell him what I think of him!' he stormed.

'Why don't you?' Mr. Lincoln agreed. 'Write it all down—do.'

Mr. Stanton wrote his letter. When it was finished he took it to the President. The President listened to it all.

'All right. Capital!' he nodded. 'And now, Stanton, what are you going to do with it?'

'Do with it? Why, send it, of course!'

'I wouldn't,' said the President. 'Throw it in the waste-paper basket.'

'But it took me two days to write—'

'Yes, yes, and it did you ever so much good. You feel better now. That is all that is necessary. Just throw it in the basket.'

After a little more expostulation, into the basket it went.

According to historian Allan Nevins, Stanton's "arbitrary temper was accentuated by his tendency to jump to conclusions. He would impetuously take a stand just to prove his authority, as he did early in the war in trying to destroy the invaluable

Sanitary Commission. It was accentuated also by his intolerant, vindictive nursing of prejudices and grudges. He almost never admitted himself wrong, tried to see a situation from an antagonist's eye, or showed generosity to a foe either victorious or defeated."

Stanton was as vehemently opposed to secession as Meigs was, dismissing all Confederate soldiers as traitors. The powerful symbolism of turning General Lee's home into a Union cemetery was not lost on either man.

The government had proved unscrupulous in its acquisition of the estate. When the U.S. Army occupied Arlington in 1861, the Lees attempted in good faith, via agent, to pay the taxes on the home despite the war. Philip R. Fendall presented himself to the commissioners in Alexandria, to pay the $92.07 on the property. But the government had refused the payment, claiming only Mr. or Mrs. Lee could rightfully pay the taxes in person. Neither Mrs. Lee nor her husband would do so, as they would of course be arrested once they set foot on Union soil. A date for the sale of Arlington was set: January 11, 1864.

That January day was a bitter cold and icy day in Washington. The river was frozen, and few people braved the streets that did not have to. "Although the auction was well attended, artic conditions seemed to chill the bidding. The sole offer came from the Federal government, which tendered $26,800 for the estate, something less than its assessed value of $34,100. The new owners intended to reserve the property 'for government use, for war, military, charitable, and educational purposes,'" according to Poole.

Through this farce of "unpaid taxes," the U.S. government had taken possession of the property.

"Because the auction was prominently reported in the local papers, it is certain that the Lees knew about it, but nowhere in their voluminous correspondence does this milestone appear to be mentioned directly," wrote Arlington historian Poole. "General Lee may have cryptically referred to the sale a few weeks after the event, when he wrote to Mary on February 6, 1864, 'I am glad you have not been discouraged by the notice in the papers.'"

On June 15, 1864, in a letter to Stanton, Meigs officially proposed Arlington as the site of the new national cemetery. Stanton approved the measure the same day. Stanton further indicated that the part of Arlington to be used to this effect should be done so, "not exceeding two hundred acres."

The Republican press hailed the choice of Arlington. On June 17, the *National Republican* reported:

> The 'powers that be' have been induced to appropriate two hundred acres, imme-

diately around the house of General Lee, on Arlington Heights, for the burial of soldiers dying in the army hospitals of this city. The grounds are undulating, handsomely adorned, and in every respect admirably fitted for the sacred purpose to which they have been dedicated. The people of the entire nation will one day, not very far distant, heartily thank the initiators of this movement. . . . This and the contraband establishment there are righteous uses of the estate of the rebel General Lee, and will never dishonor the spot made venerable by the occupation of Washington.

Meigs likely appreciated the prediction that Americans would one day "heartily thank the initiators of this movement." He viewed the creation of the cemetery as a means for restoring honor to the property, which he felt Lee had dishonored by resigning from the U.S. Army and leading the Confederate forces.

Meigs had enough humility to understand that Arlington would be open to any man who had died in the struggle—Union, Confederate, or freedman.

But while the first few graves had been placed on the outskirts of the property, Meigs was adamant that the rest of the burials take place as close as possible to Lee's home. "I have visited and inspected the grounds now used as a Cemetery upon the Arlington Estate," he wrote. "I recommend that interments in this ground be discontinued and that the land surrounding the Arlington Mansion, now understood to be the property of the United States, be appropriated as a National Cemetery, to be properly enclosed, laid out, and carefully preserved for that purpose, and that the bodies recently interred be removed to the National Cemetery thus to be established. The grounds about the Mansion are admirably adapted for such a use."

According to Arlington historian Robert Poole, "Meigs visited the new cemetery on the morning of its creation, touring the place with Edward Clark, the engineer and architect he assigned to survey the property. On the tour of Arlington, Meigs was incensed to find that his orders to cluster the graves around the Lee mansion had been ignored: most of the new burials were still being placed in the Lower Cemetery."

Meigs was beyond aggravated. He had wanted the first burials, of Christman and the others, to have been nearer the mansion. This was intolerable.

"My plans for the cemetery had been to some degree thwarted," he fumed. "It was my intention to have begun the interments nearer the mansion. But opposition from officers stationed at

Arlington—some of whom did not like to have the dead buried near them—caused the interments to be begun in the Northeastern quarter of the grounds near Alexandria road.

"On discovering this by a visit I gave special instructions to make the burials near the mansion. They were driven off by the same influence to the western portion of the grounds . . . On discovering the second error I caused the officers to be buried around the garden."

To make matters sure, Meigs evicted General René E. DeRussy and his staff, who had made the mansion their very comfortable head-quarters. He replaced them with two chaplains, who served a dual purpose: the chaplains would do as they were instructed and they could offer more conventional and religiously appropriate burials.

Meigs "then went about encircling Mary Lee's garden—where she'd liked to read in warm weather, surrounded by honeysuckle—with the graves of prominent Union officers. The first, Capt. Albert H. Packard, had been shot in the head at the Battle of the Second Wilderness," reported *Mainline Today*, a magazine. The first burials near the mansion, twenty-six in all, took place in August of 1864.

"Once Meigs had his new bureaucratic arrangements in place, Mrs. Lee's garden began to fill with graves. Union captains and lieutenants joined the handful of officers already sleeping on the hilltop, one felled by a shot to the chest, another by a thigh wound, an arm wound, a face wound, a shoulder wound, a knee wound. Others died of diphtheria, typhoid, or dysentery; others from the shock or infection from amputation. One died from drinking bad whiskey," wrote Poole.

But Meigs would have more important burials to oversee before the cemetery was finished.

The gravestones at Arlington in the old section of the Cemetery.

*A photo of John Rodgers Meigs
as a West Point Cadet.*

CHAPTER 8
DEATH COMES

It was a rainy day on October 3, 1864, when Brevet Major John Meigs and two assistants spent the afternoon mapping the area around Harrisonburg, Virginia, plotting routes for the movement of General Sheridan's troops in the

Shenandoah Valley. At dusk, Meigs and his assistants rode along a road in Swift Run Gap between Harrison and Dayton, Virginia, near where Sheridan's headquarters were located.

Young and handsome, with thick, wavy brown hair and a lean, trim build, John Rodgers Meigs was the eldest son of Montgomery C. Meigs. Young Meigs had graduated first in the West Point class of 1863 and served as a highly regarded staff engineer before joining Sheridan.

Meigs was the eldest of seven children, three of whom did not survive to adulthood. John had a violent temper and often bullied his siblings, behaviors that deeply concerned his parents.

The children of Montgomery C. Meigs.

"When words failed to stop his fighting with his siblings, his father disciplined him in a very strict manner," wrote biographer Mary A. Giunta.

"On one occasion Montgomery C. Meigs locked his son in his bedroom after he first bound his arms and then tied him 'to the leg of the wardrobe and left him there, without dinner, all the afternoon.' When he returned to the locked room and found that John had untied himself, his father whipped him with the rope."

Still, for all his faults, John was a shining star within the Meigs family. Bright, cheerful, inquisitive, and restless, he was a presence in the household, and much loved by his family and his extended family.

Because his father was a career military officer, and the family moved often, John was largely home schooled during his formative years. Despite his behavioral problems he was unusually bright. He began speaking at an early age, learned the alphabet while still very young, and was reading and writing by the age of four. The Meigs family returned to Washington, D.C. in November of 1852, after his father was assigned to design and finish the Washington Aqueduct. It was at this time that his parents finally enrolled him in school and his formal education began.

At the age of fourteen, he enrolled at Columbian College (later renamed George Washington University). After a short period he decided to seek an appointment to West Point. His mother was encouraging, but his father less so. Since he was an army officer's son, John Meigs's application would go through the secretary of war's office, to be subsequently approved by President James Buchanan.

"Several important political leaders including Jefferson Davis, Stephen A. Douglas, and R.M.T. Hunter, found John qualified and supported his application," Giunta wrote. "Davis wrote that Meigs 'possesses high mental and physical qualifications . . . He has a fondness for scientific pursuits and gives promise of a career worthy of his illustrious Grand Father Commodore.' "

Despite these glowing recommendations, Secretary of War John B. Floyd denied his application twice. John's father Montgomery and Floyd had been at odds for some time regarding the costs and contract-letting of the Washington, D.C., aqueduct. On June 23, 1859, Montgomery visited President Buchannan to try and resolve the matter. Buchannan washed his hands of it. After several months of failing to find more suitable candidates Floyd relented, and John was admitted.

"In early September 1859, Captain Montgomery C. Meigs . . . took his seventeen-year-old son, John Rodgers Meigs, to West Point to begin his military training," wrote Carol Bleser. "Not long after, Floyd 'exiled' him to the Dry Tortugas." Eventually Floyd was gone, and Meigs was recalled to Washington.

John initially found life difficult at West Point. His parents wrote him often, advising him as best they could to maintain the highest moral standards, determined work ethic, and elegant social graces. They could be very critical of him as well. His father urged him to learn Greek and Latin, and to read only the best books such as compilations of famous people's letters, histories, and novels that promoted high moral values.

*Here is a photo of West Point
as it looked in 1862.*

Young Meigs remained temperamental. In November 1860, Meigs's parents received a report from the academy informing them that their son had received seventy-four demerits. The notice reminded them that the institution's limit was one hundred demerits, with expulsion the result. John haughtily reasoned that the demerits were unfairly awarded to him. He claimed his first lieutenant disliked him and had not given him the deserved military or personal respect.

On April 12, 1861, the first shots were fired on Fort Sumter, and the war had commenced. Many teachers at the institute had resigned to take commissions in the Confederate Army. Eager cadets from West Point volunteered to fight, and the Union Army very much lacked properly trained officers. With so few officers left within the ranks of the Union Army, John urgently wanted to join the fight, if at least temporarily. John requested a furlough from his father so that he could participate in the defense of Washington, and General Meigs gave his permission. The furlough commenced on July 2 and ended on August 28. Cadet Meigs arrived at his parents' house in Washington on the morning of July 18.

On that same day Meigs arrived in Washington, he joined the newly reconstituted reserve unit, Hunt's Light Company M, 2nd United States Artillery. It was attached to General Irvin McDowell's Army of Northeastern Virginia. McDowell assigned Company M to Colonel Israel B. Richardson's 4th Brigade, Second Michigan Volunteers. Meigs's role in this unit remains unclear. Several sources, including the official U.S. Army biographical register, place him as an aide-de-camp to Colonel Richardson. However, other sources officially list him as assigned to Major Hunt's Light Company M. Whatever the confusion, it is clear that he carried orders and acted as an observer for both Hunt and Richardson.

On July 21, 1861, McDowell drove his men,

including John Meigs, across Bull Run, where P.G.T. Beauregard was waiting for them. McDowell drove Beauregard's men clear across the battlefield, and by afternoon, it seemed like the Union would fashion an easy victory. But Stonewall Jackson's group held firm, and Beauregard ordered a counter movement. By the end of the day, the rebels reversed the course of the battle completely, resulting in a massive and disastrous retreat by the Union troops. Much of the Union Army panicked and fled the field. Confusion reigned everywhere, but Meigs kept his head. In the absence of a commanding officer, he directed the fire and movement of troops as they withdrew toward Fairfax, Virginia. Without leave John returned to the capital, arriving at his parents' home at about eight a.m. He had wanted to let them know that he had not been injured. He told his father that he wanted to return to his unit, but his father insisted he report to the war department, and then immediately return to West Point. Disappointed, Meigs followed orders.

Cadet Meigs garnered glowing reports from his commanding officers. Major Hunt later wrote, "On the death of Lieutenant Craig, Cadet Meigs performed his duties until the close of action with spirit and intelligence, and was very useful, after the affair was over, in conveying orders, observing the enemy, and rallying our troops." Colonel Richardson, too, lauded him. He wrote in his after-action report, "Meigs carried my orders promptly, and a braver and more gallant young man was never in service." Richardson wrote to John's father, Montgomery, saying, the "gallant conduct of your son, and his exertions in carrying orders for me in the field . . . recommended him to be immediately made a Lieut. in the regular Army."

Secretary of War Simon Cameron offered to give John a commission as a second lieutenant, but General Meigs prevailed on the secretary to send his son back to school. Instead, Cameron wrote a glowing letter of commendation to Cadet Meigs on December 15, 1861.

Back at West Point, Meigs was appointed sergeant in the Battalion of Cadets on August 29, 1861. Two days later, he was assigned to the mathematics department under the supervision of Professor Albert E. Church.

His parents continued to stress achievement, honor, and military glory, but the refrain often fell on deaf ears. On May 17, 1862, he engaged in a fight with another cadet. Both students required hospitalization, but Meigs had received the worst of it. He was court-martialed for fighting, with a recommendation of suspension, but Secretary of War Cameron reduced it to confinement to campus for the duration of the summer. By early 1863, John was an acting assistant professor at West Point, teaching courses in calculus and surveying.

He graduated on June 11, 1863 and was immediately commissioned a first lieutenant of engineers.

Meigs's first assignment was as assistant engineer working to improve the western and southwestern defenses of Baltimore, Harpers Ferry, and Cumberland. Meigs was no stranger to engagements, and he saw active fighting throughout this period of his service. He even received a commendation from the new secretary of war Edwin M. Stanton, who hailed his accomplishments, citing "meritorious and dangerous" service.

Meigs saw action in the field at Gettysburg as well as after, following General Robert E. Lee's retreat from Pennsylvania for most of that July. He assisted in guarding the telegraph wires and roads along the B&O Railroad between Washington and Harpers Ferry, keeping communication and travel free in case Lee surged in a new direction. On July 13, near Harpers Ferry, Meigs's small unit of engineers skirmished with Lee's pickets.

In late July of that same year, he was reassigned to extensive surveying of the area. Meigs drew hundreds of topographical maps and assisted in designing and overseeing the construction of defensive works. He also reconnoitered on behalf of General William Averell's troops on several occasions. Meigs fought in the Battle of Rocky Gap on August 26 to 27, 1863, near White Sulphur Springs, West Virginia. On November 6, he

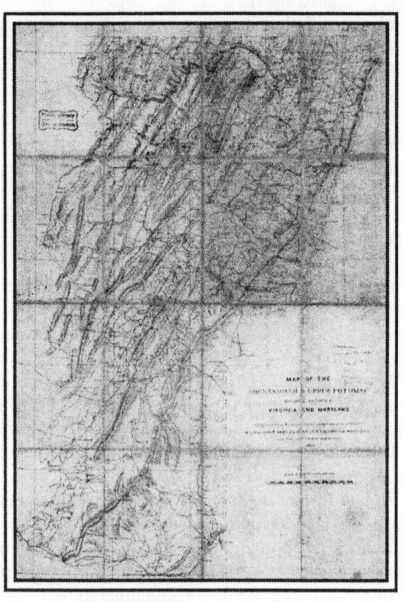

*This is a detailed map drawn by
John Rodgers Meigs who was taught to be
one of the better map makers of the
Civil War during his brief career.*

participated in the Battle of Droop Mountain in West Virginia, and the pursuit of Confederate forces after the battle from November 6 to 18. He also ordered the first shots in the "Salem Raid" on December 16.

At the start of campaigning in the spring of 1864, Lieutenant General Ulysses S. Grant was named commander of all Union Armies. Grant resolved to strike at the Confederacy on multiple fronts, including a major attack from West Virginia southwest through the Shenandoah Valley. Under Major General Franz Sigel, Meigs was named chief engineer and topographer of the Army of the Shenandoah. On May 15, 1864, Meigs was involved in combat at the Battle of New Market, a Union defeat.

Sigel was eventually replaced by Brigadier General David Hunter, who resumed the offensive and pushed toward Staunton, Virginia. Meigs led scouting parties day and night that provided crucial information. On July 3, Phillip Sheridan was named the new commander of the Union Army of the Shenandoah Valley. Sheridan believed that understanding the topography of the Shenandoah Valley would give him a strategic and tactical advantage. By the summer of 1864, Meigs was recognized as one of the best map makers in the Union Army. Meigs quickly became one of Sheridan's favorite officers. On August 17, John Rodgers Meigs was appointed Chief

Engineer of the Middle Military Division and aide-de-camp to General Sheridan.

Proud father Montgomery wrote in his diary, "John is known as the Lieut General. Hand full of maps & a head full of plans always."

The Valley Campaign opened on August 16 in the Battle of Guard Hill, when Sheridan's forces surprised Confederate General Jubal Early's cavalry riding to reinforce Early in Maryland. Early won the initial skirmishes, but Sheridan's forces began pushing south down the Shenandoah Valley again. Early and Sheridan seesawed back and forth.

On September 1, 1864, John had written a lengthy letter to his father about the battlefront, but paused, remarking wistfully, "I should think that it would be rather cool at Rye Beach now. We in camp here sleep with two blankets over us at night and feel chilly in the morning even then. The weather we are having now is the finest that can be imagined for active campaigning."

Two weeks later, he sent a letter to his mother, Louisa, writing,

> Before I got to bed I must acknowledge the receipt of your and Mary's Kind letters. It makes me quite happy to read these letters from home and see that though widely separated from you all I am still thought of.

We are going to have a terrible fight tomorrow and will have to be up at two o'clock in the morning. I feel that the chances are in our favor and if our troops behave well we must win the day and a glorious victory it will be.

Still God only knows what the result will be and if it is not for us I am afraid it will be fearfully against us.

Give my love to all!

Meigs saw combat at the Battle of Opequon on September 19, 1864, a decisive Union victory. Sheridan promoted Meigs to brevet captain the following day for his battlefield valor. John again saw action on September 21 and 22 in the Battle of Fisher's Hill. And again, Sheridan promoted him, this time to brevet major on September 22.

Sheridan's campaign "infamously became known for generations simply as 'The Burning.' The men were ordered to move fast, destroy everything that could be useful to the enemy, then move on quickly to new targets. They were instructed to spare houses, empty barns, property of widows, single women, and orphans, and to refrain from looting."

Colonel James H. Kidd of Custer's brigade described the scene as they set fire to a mill in Port Republic: "What I saw there is burned into my memory. The anguish pictured in their faces would have melted any heart not seared by the horrors and 'necessities' of war. It was too much for me and at the first moment that duty would permit I hurried from the scene." Regardless of personal feelings about the suffering of civilians, there was an element of revenge in the campaign.

General Wesley Merritt described the area as a "paradise of bushwhackers and guerrillas. Officers and men had been murdered in cold blood on the roads while proceeding without a guard through an apparently peaceful country."

"The father worried," wrote Montgomery C. Meigs's biographer, David W. Miller. "He told his father that 'though hopeful of disposition & temperament,' he felt it possible that they may have received the last letter that they would ever receive from John. Since the war began, he prayed twice a day to the Almighty on John's behalf."

Meanwhile, determined to attack Sheridan, General Early called a council of his lieutenants and it was decided to send two trusted scouts to Bridgewater to see if it was possible to obtain information of the expected move of Sheridan, and also to locate his position.

"On the morning of October 3, 1864, a man from North Carolina named Campbell and one from East Virginia named Martin, members of Rosser's brigade, were detailed to perform this duty. Inasmuch as they were not familiar with the roads in that section, an officer in the 1st Va. said he would get a man that lived there and knew every pig trail to accompany them. Forthwith he sent for B. Frank Shaver, Co. I, 1st Va." wrote Peter Cline Kaylor, in 1925, of the incident.

"Shaver, born and reared on the farm now owned by Q. G. Kaylor, had little more than reached his majority when Virginia called for troops. He volunteered in the cavalry and developed at once into a fearless and adventurous soldier. He took to scout duty as naturally as a duck takes to water. He was a splendid type of physical manhood—more than six feet in height, of dark complexion, with black hair and beard," wrote Kaylor.

"Shaver had never met Martin and Campbell until this trip. When informed of his task he was pleased. He said, 'I would like to go home and see the folks and get a good square meal.' He also remarked that he had received a letter from his sister Hannah stating that they had a Federal guard with them, and that he would probably have a Yankee brother-in-law when he returned home. Imagining that this guard had probably spoken to some of the family about the Federal movements and that this would be an ideal place to get infor-mation the trio started. Arriving at Bridgewater and learning nothing of Sheridan's movements, they decided to go through the picket posts to Shaver's home, having learned where the several pickets were stationed."

*John Rodgers Meigs in his
Union Army uniform.*

On that rainy day on October 3, 1864, Brevet Major John Meigs and two assistants were returning to camp via Swift Run Gap road between Harrison and Dayton, Virginia. They had been out all day, and it was dusk when they saw a small posse of men dressed in dark coats that may have appeared blue. Both groups were wearing rain ponchos that covered their uniforms and made it difficult to identify which army each belonged to.

Assuming the men to be Union troops, Meigs rode into their midst. In reality, they were three Confederate scouts guided by local resident Private Shaver, attached to a brigade commanded by Brigadier General Williams Carter Wickham.

These Confederates had entered behind the Union lines that morning to observe the dispositions of Sheridan's army camped around Harrisonburg. Upon recognizing one another, each group demanded that the other surrender.

Frank Shaver later corroborated what the second Union topographer reported. Meigs had fired first. Shaver claimed Meigs was given fair warning that they were Confederates, but charged at them anyway.

In a flash, both sides drew aim. Suddenly the air was alive with firearm reports and whistling lead. Meigs wounded a scout. But the rebels countered, and returned fire. Shavers stated that he shot Meigs in the head, while Private F.M. Campbell shot Meigs in the chest. Meigs tumbled off his horse and landed on the muddy ground. He was dead.

One of the assistants was captured and the other fled, riding all the way back to General Sheridan's headquarters to report the engagement. The fleeing assistant reported to Sheridan that they had been "bushwhacked." This was understandable given that all were wearing rain slickers, and it was dusk, and the Confederates might not have been wearing uniforms given their scouting was taking place behind enemy lines. However, the assistant embellished the story, telling the general that Meigs had been shot in cold blood, unarmed, and crying, "Don't shoot me!" Why he told this story was never known. Sheridan was enraged.

"Sheridan had believed that Meigs had fallen victim to Confederate partisans. Incensed, Sheridan ordered the village of Dayton, Virginia, in the central Shenandoah Valley burned to the ground in retaliation. He also ordered all homes and buildings destroyed within a five-mile radius of Dayton," wrote historian Paul G. Pierpaoli Jr.

Edwin Stanton was informed of the news by General Sheridan, and he took it upon himself to tell Montgomery and Louisa Meigs personally. "Stanton came to the Meigs' home and asked Montgomery to come outside," wrote Miller. The portly secretary of war, with his great bushy beard, waited outside for Meigs to come down the front stairs of his house. "[Meigs's] initial thought was that Stanton had bad tidings—maybe that it was that Grant had fallen, or a dreadful fate had befallen the President. Alas, it was news that 22-year-old John Rodgers Meigs was dead."

"About this hour my son, 1st Lt. John Rodgers Meigs Corps of U.S. Engineers, while in discharge of his duty reconnoitering near General Sheridans Head Quarters and a little south of Harrisonburg, Va. was killed by guerillas. . . ." Meigs recorded in his diary the next day. Major General George A. "Sandy" Forsyth ". . . went out and found the body of my son where he had fallen unrifled, the left arm raised, the right extended at his side. He lay upon his short cape or cloak, a bullet through the head and another through the heart."

With nothing but his classic Puritan background to uphold him, Meigs stoically wrote that he found "much consolation in the memory of good deeds faithful service heroic endeavor and patriotic self-sacrifice."

On October 5 he wrote, "And so perishes my first born a noble boy, gallant, generous, gifted who had already made a name for himself. At the age of 19 he had fought with distinction at the first battle of war Bull Run, 21 July 61. He had been in most active service since he graduated in July 63, and had passed through many battles unscathed a martyr in the cause of Liberty."

The news of the "murder" of Montgomery Meigs's son swept the nation, and newspapers in the North shouted for justice and revenge. The wire John himself had guarded now carried the news of his death throughout the country.

Wickham, realizing whom his men had killed, released his prisoner and sent him back to Sheridan in the hope that the Union soldier would report a more accurate version of the story. This second assistant told Sheridan that the Confederates pulled their guns first and captured Meigs and his men. With his cape concealing his movements, Meigs pulled his pistol out and shot Private George Martin. Martin and the uninjured Confederates then shot Meigs dead.

Brigadier General Montgomery C. Meigs was devastated by his son's death and determined to seek justice. "Meigs' father believed that his son's death had been premeditated murder, and offered a $1,000 reward for the apprehension of his son's killer," wrote Pierpaoli. This fueled the flames of the headlines in the press even further.

The New York Times reported on Friday, October 7, 1864:

> A dispatch from Gen. STEVENSON reports that an officer of Gen. SHERIDAN's Staff had just arrived. Gen. SHERIDAN was still at Harrisonburgh. His supply trains were going on all right, occasionally interrupted by guerrilla parties, the only rebel force on the road.
>
> This officer brought in the remains of Lieut. JOHN R. MEIGS, of the Engineer Corps, the only son of Brevet Maj.-Gen. MEIGS, Quartermaster-General. He was killed by bushwhackers on Monday last, while making a military survey. In the death of this gallant young officer the department has occasion to deplore no ordinary loss. Last year he graduated at the Military Academy of West Point with the highest honors, at the head of his class. He was commissioned Lieutenant of Engineers, and immediately went into the

field. He performed meritorious and distinguished services during the campaigns of last year on the fortifications at Baltimore, Harpers Ferry and Cumberland, and was made Chief of Engineers of the Army of the Shenandoah. In the campaigns he accompanied the army under SIGEL, HUNTER and SHERIDAN. In every position he gave proof of great professional skill, personal courage and devoted patriotism. One of the youngest and brightest ornaments of the military profession, he has fallen an early victim to the murderous rebel warfare.

The New York Times also carried a later dispatch from the war department, wherein Sheridan reported to Sherman:

> In moving back to this point the whole country from the Blue Ridge to the North Mountain has been made entirely untenable for a rebel army.
> I have destroyed over two thousand barns filled with wheat and hay and farming implements, over seventy mills filled with flour and wheat; have driven in front of the army over four thousand head of stock, and have killed and issued to the troops not less than 3,000 sheep.

This destruction embraces the Luray Valley and Little Fort Valley, as well as the main Valley.

A large number of horses have been obtained, a proper estimate of which I cannot now make.

Lieut. JOHN R. MEIGS, my Engineer officer, was murdered beyond Harrison-burgh, near Dayton. For this atrocious act all the houses within an area . . . were burned.

Since I came into the Valley from Harpers Ferry, every train, every small party, and every straggler, has been bushwhacked by the people, many of whom have protection-passes from commanders who have been hitherto in that valley.

The people here are getting sick of the war. Heretofore they have had no reason to complain, because they have been living in great abundance.

These reports on Meigs's death were repeated in countless newspapers across the country.

"The following day residents of Dayton were warned of the impending destruction and moved their property and families into the surrounding lots and fields, where they spent the night, waiting to see their homes go up in flames. In the mean-time news of the burnings that took place the same evening that Meigs was killed and the information that Dayton was to be destroyed as soon as the women, children, and old men were moved out, had reached the Confederate forces," Kaylor continued.

According to Kaylor:

The evening Dayton was to be burned (the day after Meigs's death), the Federal soldiers helped move the household goods from the dwellings into the surrounding fields and lots where it would be out of danger of the fires. That evening, when the order to burn was revoked, it was too late to move back into the houses; so the Federal officer in charge placed guards with each family to protect them from that class of rough-necks that are in all armies.

When Sheridan received orders to destroy the grain and other supplies that were stored in mills and barns, and was carrying out the order by applying the torch the burners came to the Burkholder farm, near Garber's Church, to destroy the barn, which contained grain. The wind being strong, and blowing towards the residence, they went away and left it, for fear of destroying the house. This occurred a few days after the burnings around

Dayton, on the death of Meigs. Sheridan began his retreat and burning down the Valley about October 5.

At the borne of Joel Flory, father of Jacob Flory, east of Dayton, on the Pike Church Road, old Aunt Betsy Whitmore was lying bedfast at the time the Yankees came to burn the house. After learning the condition of Aunt Betsy they went off and did no burning. A similar situation was found at Abraham Paul's, where the barn was burned, but not the residence, because in the latter was a sick woman (a Miss Paul).

Destruction of supplies was the object in the general burning, not the destruction of buildings. This was shown at the mill of Gen. Sam Lewis, at Lynnwood. This mill had a large quantity of wheat in it, but news was sent by "grape-vine telegraph" to General Lewis (who was a Union man) that if the grain were taken out before morning the mill would not be burned, He had his son, the late Sen. John F. Lewis, who was then superintendent of Mt. Vernon Iron Works, to send the furnace teams down and haul out the wheat during the night. This mill was not burned. Neither were some other mills and barns that were empty.

Sheridan soon rescinded the order concerning Dayton. By then approximately thirty dwellings had been razed in what came to be known as the "Burnt District."

Kaylor wrote of Martin, the wounded Confederate, was operated on for his wound, "under the skillful hands of Dr. Brown and his nurses, was soon able to return to his home, but he did not see service again as a soldier. He always claimed that he had killed Meigs. About 1877 he learned that his pistol did not go off when it was aimed at Meigs's heart. When his pistol and belt were taken off they were placed on Meigs's white-faced horse and taken into Shaver's camp. Upon examination, it was found that his pistol contained all the loads, but the caps were all burst. Both Martin and Shaver had aimed at Meigs. Campbell fired at the soldier that surrendered and at the one that climbed the fence and ran into the woods. Shaver never saw Martin again after leaving him at Robert Wright's, nor Campbell after they separated at Shaver's camp, until about 1878. Then the three met in Richmond by appointment. Shaver remained in the army until the surrender. He was paroled, came home, and resumed work on his father's farm. The general amnesty granted to Confederate soldiers by the Federal government did not apply to him because he, Martin, and Campbell had gone inside the enemy's lines at the time Lieut. Meigs was killed; so they were considered as spies."

The site of John Rodgers Meigs's death.

After the war, the three Confederates whom Meigs had encountered that day swore that the fight had been fair and that Meigs was amply warned of their intentions. In a 1914 article the *Confederate Veteran* magazine carefully reconstructed the events surrounding Meigs's death and concluded that nothing untoward had happened when he was shot and killed. "One of thousands of such incidents during the war, this event became infamous because of the victim's familial celebrity and social standing," concluded historian Paul G. Pierpaoli Jr.

After his death, John Rodgers Meigs received a posthumous promotion to the rank of major. He was buried with full military honors.

John Rodgers Meigs's body was temporarily

housed in the chapel at Oak Hill Cemetery in Washington, D.C. while a fresh grave was dug. The twenty-two-acre cemetery was located in the Georgetown neighborhood and had been recently completed in 1853. The Oak Hill Chapel is a pretty, Gothic revival style brownstone church with touches of white tracery. It was surrounded by much greenery. In mid-October, the trees would have been gorgeous in their mid-fall display.

The Oak Hill Cemetery Chapel in Washington, D.C. where Meigs's body was housed.

President Abraham Lincoln, Secretary of State William H. Seward, Secretary of War Edwin M. Stanton, Army Chief-of-Staff Lieutenant General Henry Halleck, and numerous other dignitaries attended Meigs's funeral. The tiny chapel was filled with the powerful of Washington. "One of the youngest and brightest of the military profession," Stanton said in his eulogy, "he has fallen an early victim to murderous rebel warfare."

It took a long time for the Meigs family to recover. Louisa, Montgomery's wife, wrote her sister Ann Minerva "Nannie" Rogers Macon, "When I look back over the years that have passed when God first gave him to me, how short and how precious they seem, how little I anticipated the aging in store for me when I bid you adieu so short a time since. I have been crushed to the earth. I begin to look up and feel that my duties to the living must be done . . . how vain, all life seems. My daring precious John, I seem to hear his step in the hall, & I see his bright happy face as I last saw him, and I crave to be alone, to sit and think of the past . . ." In another letter to Nannie she pointed out, "I do not know how I should have sustained myself in this dreadful grief without my dear Husband to lean upon. He has been a source of strength to me. His cheerful submission to God's will is beautiful & wonderful, seeing how proud he was of his son and how much he loved him. He feels that he died a martyr in the great cause of human liberty, and could not have perished more nobly. He does not [illegible] though he had moments of dreadful grief."

However, in Montgomery C. Meigs there was a profound change. Meigs was inconsolable. As historian Russell F. Weigley wrote, with the loss of his son, "his consequent embitterment sealed his political transformation from pre-war Democrat to a Republican of Radical inclination, favoring land redistribution for the freedmen. It also inspired him in his efforts to make Robert E. Lee's estate at Arlington into a national cemetery . . . Formally an Episcopalian, Meigs retained an ethical code reminiscent of his Puritan forebears in its combination of stern, inner-directed demands on himself with a humorless self-righteousness."

Even President Abraham Lincoln, as well as many of his cabinet members, attended the funeral services of John Rodgers Meigs. This photo was taken February 5, 1865, and is generally considered the last photo of Lincoln taken in life.

General Robert E. Lee, 1869.

CHAPTER 9

SEARCHING FOR ARLINGTON

From the war's end until the time of her death, Mary Anna Randolph Custis Lee never stopped trying to recoup the possessions most important to her from her years at Arlington, including the estate itself. Her correspondence shows a soul strong in faith trying to piece back her life after the travesty of war.

"Mary lost no time in applying for the return of Arlington," wrote Mary's biographer John Perry. "But despite the tenuous legality of the government's wartime confiscation, popular opinion in Washington was dead set against returning it." On May 25, 1865, under the headline "Arlington and Mrs. General Lee" the *Washington Daily Morning Chronicle* declared:

> Mrs. Lee, the wife of the rebel leader, Robert E. Lee, has formally announced her determination to lay claim to Arlington Heights, and is in a very ill humor because that baronial estate has not been sufficiently cared for by the vile Yankees . . . There is in the vicinity of Arlington House, indeed on the part of the property, a romantic spot in which some hundreds of Union heroes murdered by the orders of Mrs. Lee's husband, or by her husband's troops, are buried. These sacred remains shall not be profaned by the unhallowed touch, much less outraged by the usurping demands, of this race of savages and traitors. Heaven save the nation from the humiliation!

On July 1, Mary, the General, and Custis sat down together in the small Derwent house on the large Oakland plantation in Cumberland County, owned by Edmund R. Cocke. It was a lovely home, though nowhere near the grandeur of Arlington. But for the first time since the war, the Lee family was together. "After a warm welcome, the Lee family sat down to a bountiful breakfast reminiscent of the old days at Arlington: ham, sausage, broiled tomatoes, and four kinds of bread," wrote Perry

Mary wrote to a friend on September 21, 1865, "My heart yearns to be at the home of my youth, The most beloved spot on earth to me, and the knowledge of how it is occupied and desecrated is a bitter grief to me. Yet I shall never rest until it is restored, nor will I ever relinquish my claim to it."

But time passed, and with it, Mary's rheumatism grew worse. Her son Robert spent the summer recovering from malaria and a severe case of poison ivy. He recalled years later that she was by that time what many would consider to be an invalid. She used a wheelchair more often than not, and could wheel herself around on even floors, but her strength had been sapped. However, Robert concluded, "she was always bright, sunny-tempered, and uncomplaining, constantly occupied with her books, letters, knitting, and painting, for the last of which she had great talent."

Nevertheless, late 1865 found General Lee and Mary living in Lexington, Virginia, far away from the hue and cry of either Washington or

Richmond. In this sleepy little college town, Robert accepted the position of president of Washington College. He would stay there the rest of his life.

General Lee had gone ahead in September to take up the position at Washington College and prepare the house for them to live in. It was some months before Mary joined him. But she never let go of her wish to regain her old home. If she could not have Arlington itself, in the short term, then she could regain her lost or stolen possessions.

The President's House, at Washington and Lee University, as it stands today.

"I expect to join my husband at Lexington on Tuesday next and have been prevented doing so before by the delays he has experienced in preparing the house for our reception. We shall at least have a house for the present thus I feel much like an exile until I get back to my beloved Arlington," she wrote to Mrs. H.R. Glenn, of Baltimore, Maryland on November 23, 1865.

"Despite every effort to speed the work on the house, it was not ready for the Lees to occupy until the beginning of December," wrote Lee biographer Michael Korda. "They had not had a home of their own since 1861, and their furniture and their possessions were scattered. Lee managed to recover the carpets from Arlington; these had been saved and stored at Tudor Place, across the Potomac in Georgetown heights," by Mrs. Kennon, a descendent of George Washington and a distant relation to Mary.

"Although they were much too large, even with their edges folded back, for the rooms of 'The Presidential Residence on College Hill,' they at least provided a touch of luxury and a faint reminder of Arlington. Mrs. Cocke had provided some of the furniture and an admirer had provided a piano. The Lee family silver, which had been providentially sent to Lexington for safe keeping and buried, was soon unearthed and laboriously cleaned," concluded Korda.

Showing a flash of his old humor, Lee himself later wrote of the looters and the scattered artifacts of Arlington, "I hope the possessors appreciate them and may imitate the example of their original owners, whose conduct must at times be brought to their recollection by these silent monitors. In this way they will accomplish good to the country."

Almost a year later Mary wrote to a family friend with a list of things she was hoping still to recover, including two mahogany knife cases, an old fashioned washstand, green silk window curtain fringes, white hooked curtains and counterpane, blankets, the Washington coat of arms, old andirons, an old Stick Chair, one large china bowl, one green China teapot (and two others), three glass finger bowls, and her Cincinnati china (including forty plates, ten flat dishes, seven deep dishes, and six small pieces).

"My cousin Miss Heather Williams who lived with us at Arlington many years, will leave here Monday for George Town and will confer with you on the subject of the removal of our property," she wrote to a friend on September 12, 1866. "She will also go over to Arlington where she left many articles of her own with full authority from me to take anything she desires to. Mrs. Kennon is in George Town. We have a faithful woman who is still at Arlington who was left in charge of the house, Selena Grey, who can give more information concerning all that is contained than anyone else and who in vain exerted herself to save what was so dear to me from destruction—I am particularly anxious to recover my family Bible and a very old one with clasps. The frames of all my pictures which I left hanging on the walls of the rooms and which could have been of little value to anyone else, a small Mexican saddle mounted with silver left in the garret and a large package sewed up in linen containing very handsome crimson silk brocade curtains and an old fashioned brocade—of my grandmother—all our house silver—I mention these things because Colonel Taylor was kind enough to say that he would institute some search for things that were missing."

Gathering her things was as close as she could get to regaining Arlington itself, and it became her newfound goal. This would take her years to accomplish.

"I have been hoping everyday my dear friend to hear again from my cousin Miss Williams concerning my dear house & know if there was any hope of recovering those things which have been abstracted by the different officers stationed at Arlington who I suppose should would be glad to deliver them up to me to whom alone they are of inestimable value. I especially refer to my books which I hear were packed up and carried away by Lt Master Ingalls, all my house linens, many articles from Mt. Vernon are said to have been taken [by] General Major Banks. I knew nothing of the facts of the case but only that these things are gone. If you think there is any hope of recovering them I can send you a list," Mary wrote P.A. Fendall, in Washington from their home in Lexington on October 12, 1866.

"Colonel Taylor has expressed much sympathy in my wrongs that he may perhaps aid me in regard to the things taken from Arlington—What has been saved is of little value save from association. Will you present us most kindly? To you for those exertions I shall ever remember with gratitude. You may think it strange I should not have secured all moveable articles before I left Washington, but I had such confidence in the honor of the U.S. Officers. I thought the place would be guarded, respected and also hoped to return in a few days or weeks and secure the many things which I left ere this was accomplished I heard the place was occupied by U.S. troops."

She wrote to Fendall a month later, on November 12, from Lexington to Washington, "Upon reflection I have determined that under order obtained for me thro' the kindness of the President it would be best to secure my property new in the Patent Office of which I enclose a list tho' it may not be a correct one as it was taken hastily while on a visit there. My daughter Mary wrote to Colonel Hancock Taylor on this subject but having received no reply feared that letter had not reached him, Perhaps you better consult with him and write me what you think had best be done and I can ask my cousin Mrs. Kennon to receive the relics as she has offered to take charge of them. Perhaps as they have been taken away from Arlington without my wish or permission the department will deliver them to Mrs. Kennon."

A month later she asked for more pieces, and yet, it had been determined that the new house could not hold all of Arlington's furniture. Some of the items from their old estate would have to be put up for sale.

Only three weeks later, she wrote again to Fendall, "I only have a few moments to reply to your very kind letter and I am anxious you should receive this before you send the articles I wrote for—If they have not already started will you add it to those hanging book shelves and if among the books you see a Latin and French dictionary and a small volume of Horace bound in paper and presented to me by my father, I would be much obliged if you would add them to the collection also any Bible or Prayer Book—It would be scarcely worthwhile to send all those Books here at present as it would be attended with much expense and we have but little room for them . . ."

She concluded, "I must thank you for so promptly settling all the charges of the cabmen and will send the amount as soon as I find a safe opportunity of doing so, unless in the mean time you should be able to dispose of any of my furniture to that amount any of those washstands except the oak set you can sell if for their value at all. And there is a high post mahogany bedstead carved and very handsome your Father sent to Old Point for me when I was married which I would like to keep. Any other of the walnut furniture can be sold—I enclose a note to Mr. Muir which you will please give and look at the Butlers tray and stand in his shop. If it was made at your establishment I have no doubt it is mine and shall claim it. The other articles I suspect from the description belong to my sister. . . ."

Robert E. Lee served as the president of Washington University until his death, after which the school was re-named Washington and Lee University.

Long after their move to Lexington, Mary continued to fight for her family's relics. The Washington memorabilia, which had been on display in the U.S. Patent Office, could be seen there as late as 1883. The list of items included his personal household effects, such as furniture, china, and silver, as well as his camp equipage, several uniforms, and his leather traveling desk. In 1869, there had been a gentleman's agreement by President Andrew Johnson to return the property to her, but radicals on Capitol Hill reversed the President's request on the last day before his administration was concluded. The government never returned the property to the Lee family, and instead, the assets were eventually turned over to the Smithsonian Institution where they remain today.

Mary's new position as wife of a college president preoccupied her to a certain extent. She enthusiastically courted faculty and students alike. Despite being wheelchair bound, she became known for her great hospitality, impeccable appearance, and cheerful attitude. She was always seeing to the needs of others. Still, she felt pangs of loneliness. She was far from Arlington, and just as far from the family and friends she had known all her life.

"I am still confined mostly to my chair and through the kindness of friends have found many comforts," she wrote her friend Varina Davis, the wife of imprisoned former Confederate President Jefferson Davis, on March 10, 1867. "But my heart yearns for the home and scenes of my past life. I feel as a stranger and exile, always looking forward to some change in my condition . . . Much as I long to go there, I dread to witness the plunder and desecration of my once cherished and beautiful home. I only wish I had set a torch to it when I left, or that it was sunk in the bottom of the Potomac, than used as it now is."

George Washington's marquee tent, photographed here in 1909, was one of the family's artifacts which was never returned.

The Civil War's Tomb of the Unknown Soldier
designed and built by Meigs, placed where
Mary Anna Randolph Custis Lee's
rose garden had been.

CHAPTER 10
THE TOMB OF THE UNKNOWN SOLDIER

There was no question the Lees, in the post-war years, would fight for the return of Arlington.

A cousin had written to Mary not long after Appomattox, urging her to return home: "It is thought well for persons who have property in that part of the state to be near at hand, that they may take possession as soon as it is vacated . . . I trust dear Cousin you will be back ere long at

Arlington too. I cannot believe that you will be defrauded of it."

"I cannot write with composure of my own cherished Arlington," Mary wrote of the graves. "They are even planted up to the very door without any regard to common decency . . . My heart will never know rest or peace while my dear home is so used and I am almost maddened daily by the accounts I read in the paper of the number of interments continually placed there . . . If justice and law are not utterly extinct in the U.S. I will have it back."

But Meigs seemed just as determined to prevent even the possibility of the Lees' return.

"Among Lee's adversaries, no one seemed keener to make an example of him than Meigs, still indignant over the death of his son six months before," wrote Poole.

"The rebels are all murderers of my son and the sons of hundreds of thousands," Meigs fumed, even as news of Lee's surrender reached him. "Justice seems not satisfied [if] they escape judicial and trial and execution . . . by the government which they have betrayed attacked and whose people loyal and disloyal they have slaughtered."

This letter, directed to Major General D.H. Rucker, the chief quartermaster of Washington from Col. J.M. Moore, Dec. 11, 1865 read in part: "The Quartermaster General . . . some time ago, expressed his regret, that the interments have not been made in close proximity to the Arlington House . . . as to more firmly secure the grounds known as the National Cemetery, to the Government by rendering it undesirable as a future residence or homestead. There being more than a thousand interments yet to be made, the views of the Quartermaster General can now be carried out."

According to National Parks historians at Arlington, "To underscore the urgency and importance of burying the dead close to the house, the Assistant Quartermaster closed his letter by relaying the following story: A brother of Genl. Lee (Smith Lee) in a recent visit to Arlington, remarked to the Superintendent, 'that the house could still be made a pleasant residence, by fencing off the Cemetery, and removing the officers buried around the garden.' "

By August, while the government and the Lees were still playing a chess match regarding the return of the property to the Lee family, Meigs made the ultimate move.

"When General Meigs finally received word, on September 21, 1866, that recovery crew had gathered in the last of the unknowns from Manassas and other nearby battlefields, he asked that a large shipment of them be sent to Arlington for reburial. He set laborers to work excavating a huge pit just to the southwest of Mrs. Lee's garden. Twenty feet deep and twenty around, it was to be a mass grave, which the quartermaster intended as Arlington's first memorial to unknown soldiers," wrote Poole.

"A more terrible spectacle can hardly be conceived than is to be seen within a dozen rods of the Arlington mansion," wrote a reporter of the awful spectacle for the *Washington National Intelligencer*. "Down into this gloomy receptacle are cast the bones of such soldiers as perished on the field and either were not buried at all or were so covered up as to have their bones mingle indiscriminately together. At the time we looked into this gloomy cavern, a literal Golgotha, there were piled together, skulls in one division, legs in another, arms in another, and ribs in another, what were estimated as the bones of two thousand human beings." Meigs had given an official number of 2,111. Eventually the vault was sealed, and a giant white marble sarcophagus was placed on top, designed by Meigs himself.

"By his placement of this monument, Meigs was erecting another barrier to the Lees' return. Other motives—including a sense of duty and a particular passion for design—also may have inspired his gesture, typical of much that the quartermaster initiated on the Lee estate," commented Poole.

With the construction of the tomb, Arlington's fate was sealed.

The Colonial Revival flower garden at Arlington House at Arlington National Cemetery in Virginia. With its low, walled box gardens and winding paths, it was a soothing place for Lee and his family. It is still preserved today.

The Tomb of the Unknown Dead of the Civil War contains the remains of more than 2,000 men who lost their lives that could not be accounted for or identified.

*Mary Anna Randolph Custis Lee
in her later years.*

CHAPTER 11
HER LAST VISIT

In June 1873, Mary Anna Randolph Custis Lee's coach approached the entrance to Arlington. She was sixty-four years old. It had been a dozen years since she had seen her home.

"Her features much resemble those of Martha Washington," a newspaperman wrote. "With her sad yet firm expression of face and eyes, beautiful and sparkling with the uncommon intelligence which marks her conversation; with her almost snowy white hair, fine, soft and in waves and curls, framing her full forehead, and covered by her plain widow's cap, she sits before one a grand a lovely lady."

She had by this time lost everything. And of all her most prized possessions, the general's death, three years earlier, had seemed the final blow.

According to her biographer, John Perry, "In 1870, General Lee had made a valedictory tour, greeting old friends, visiting places dear to him, and making his peace in the world. In the spring of 1873, Mary Custis Lee set out on a valedictory tour of her own.

"It was her first visit to the region since the war, and Mary received a deluge of visitors," continued Perry. "Vast numbers of friends and admirers from Virginia and Washington called, unable to imagine they would ever have the chance to see Mrs. General Lee again."

Once, as the young mistress of Arlington, her days had been filled with countless strings of relatives, girlfriends, and male admirers. She had been considered both shockingly forthright and one of the most desirable women in Virginia. Now, again, there were numerous relatives, friends, acquaintances, and political people to see.

Her visit was front-page news in the June 12, 1873 *Alexandria Gazette*. She was indeed a celebrity. "She is a lady whose noble character and Christian graces render her an object of reverence to all who meet her. Her mind is richly stored with the recollections of the patriotic, cultivated and distinguished persons who will ever be prominent in our national history. . . ."

"I was so constantly occupied in seeing my many old friends that I had scarcely a moment to myself," she later wrote of that visit. "It was a great satisfaction to me to be so warmly received by them, and not the less so that I know I am united in their hearts with the love and veneration they have borne to General Lee."

Despite the emotional turmoil that Mary must have felt, she remained composed, dignified, and gracious throughout her trip. "The pure and lofty womanhood and the true nature of Mrs. Lee's character was revealed in the farther fact that she conversed upon the whole matter without one single expression or shade of bitterness," a local newspaper reported. "Of the President and his administration she spoke in the sincerest terms of respect, and seemed entirely calm and patient in the reflection of the proper time that right would prevail. Like her great husband, she 'recognizes no necessity for the state of things' that existed when the late war commenced, and now she recognizes no necessity for any other state of things than that of the profound peace, amity and concord between the North and South."

Of her recollections, she wrote, "[There are] no illusions to the present state of that home . . . or of the agony endured by the sole survivor of that family once beloved and honored . . . It seems to me almost like a terrible dream—the present occupation and condition of that place. It is rarely out of my thoughts waking or sleeping and the longing I have to revisit is almost more than I can endure."

The Lees' former servant Selina Gray had written Mary in 1872, describing the estate to her. "Your things at the time of the war was taken away by every body," she wrote.

As Robert E. Lee biographer Douglas Southall Freeman pointed out, the family had been reunited with Washington's silver service, and nearly all the family's portraits had been removed to Tudor Place, Georgetown, and had also been forwarded after the war. But a number of Washington relics had been left at the mansion in 1861. "Some of them were stolen or carried away by individuals, as were the small personal belongings of the Lees, found in the house by marauding Federal soldiers . . . To save the remaining effects of Washington, General McDowell removed them to the department of the Interior. Placed on exhibit at the Patent Office, with the legend, 'Captured at Arlington,' they constituted a rather pitiful display—a pair of candelabra, a part of a set of china that Lafayette had given Mrs. Washington, a punch bowl, a looking-glass, a washstand, a 'dressing bureau,' a few of Washington's tent poles and pins, a little of his bed clothing and a pair of his breeches, with a waistcoat."

"One artifact of old Arlington remained, however," wrote Poole. "A rose bush Mrs. Lee had planted by her mother's grave in the hills behind the house. Mrs. Gray clipped a bud from the plant and folded it into her letter that autumn, along with this wish: 'I trust I may see the day yet when you all will have Arlington.'"

Mary now stared out at the landscape. The once proud driveway of large trunked trees was gone. In its place the drive was studded with heavy, massive stumps, like sentinels in a desolate landscape. As she went up the drive further she could see the Freedman's Village, which now housed more than two thousand former slaves, now awaiting their own fates.

"Then she saw the graves—row upon row of them with simple marble tombstones, their ranks extending out of sight," wrote Mary Custis Lee's biographer John Perry.

"I rode out to my dear old home, so changed it seemed but a dream of the past. I could not have realized that it was Arlington but for a few old oaks they had spared, and the trees planted on the lawn by the General and myself which are raising their tall branches to the Heaven which seems to smile on the desecration around them," she wrote to her friend Elizabeth Cocke on June 20, 1873.

The carriage wound its way up the drive to the mansion. The familiar columns, and large, opulent windows seemed to soothe her, but the hand-painted sign hanging over the front door, reading "cemetery office," was jarring. The garden, a tangled mess, held some semblance of its former majesty, but it was obvious that it received much less care these days than it did in the time when she, her mother, and her sisters looked after it.

The carriage paused in front of the great portico.

"Old servants ran out to meet Mary, tears streaming unchecked down their cheeks. Their familiar faces recalled a bond from another era— a bond of mutual trust, respect, and love that had outlasted any bond recognized by law," wrote John Perry. Those with Mary got up out of the carriage and walked around, stretching their legs and inspecting other nooks and crannies of the estate. But Mary remained seated in the carriage. It was painfully clear that this was no longer her Arlington. Who were these strangers walking around the estate? These soldiers? She continued to engage with the old servants and the few other faces she recognized, as other onlookers stared at the old woman.

She was offered a cup of water, and her two hands, withered and misshapen, crippled by arthritis, clutched at the vessel.

"Mary savored every swallow, every drop, the taste and smell bringing to mind her earliest memories," wrote Perry. Images of relatives long gone. Mother. Father. Robert. Children playing. The legendary gardens at their peak. After drinking, she handed back the cup and paused. She bid all the familiar faces good-bye. She slowly lifted her tired, shaky arm, and the coach lurched forward.

Despite well wishes and shouts and whispers, and teary eyes, she did not look back. The estate's road gave way to Arlington's roads, and the mansion was gone behind them—gone forever.

"My visit produced one good effect," she wrote to a friend that same week. "The change is so entire I have not the yearning to go back there and shall be more content to resign all my right in it."

Mary Anna Randolph Custis Lee never saw Arlington again. She died on November 5, 1873, little more than four months later.

Mary Anna Randolph Custis Lee never got to see the restoration of her home. But today it is fully restored to all its former glory. This is the first floor family room at Arlington as it looked during her time of residence.

John Rodgers Meigs's burial site at Arlington National Cemetery near the sarcophagus of his father Montgomery C. Meigs.

CHAPTER 12

THE FINAL RESTING PLACE

Between 1870 and 1880 Meigs made numerous suggestions to allow others to be buried in Arlington, extending it to politicians, judges, civil servants, etc. Many of these were rejected. ". . . [B]ut the existing rules did not keep him from having the remains of his grandfather (Josiah) and an uncle (Samuel Meigs) transferred from a Washington cemetery to Arlington. They died before 1823. This transfer took place after the death of Louisa Meigs in 1879. Also moved to the same location was their son John and their other three children who died before them." Several other of Meigs's family were buried with him.

Montgomery, Louisa, John, and the others are buried next to Arlington Mansion in Grave No. 1, in Section No. 1, right off of Meigs Drive. The site is marked by a giant white marble sarcophagus that displays Montgomery C. Meigs's name and accomplishments on one side, with the names of others in his family etched on the other.

The grave of John Rodgers Meigs lies a few feet away from his father's. It is a high polished square slab, roughly the size of an altar found in a church, and on it is a bronze sculpture of John Rodgers Meigs. He lies there in his soldier's uniform, just as described by Major General George A. "Sandy" Forsyth: "He had fallen unrifled, the left arm raised, the right extended at his side. He lay upon his short cape or cloak, a bullet through the head and another through the heart."

Impressions of the muddy boot prints of the Confederates surround his head and body, preserved in green tinted bronze. His pistol is just inches from him, with one chamber spent, to show he went down fighting. It is one of the most visited graves at Arlington.

There lies Montgomery Meigs's anger and pride and hurt and affection on display for all the world to see. He, like so many others, lost his son.

John Rodgers Meigs's dramatic likeness, carved as he might have looked when he fell, is one of the most visited graves in the cemetery, and displays with it the heart of a grieved father.

EPILOGUE

The Lee family would continue to fight the United States government for possession of Arlington, losing that battle in the court of opinion and on the floor of the United States Senate. In 1870, after the death of the general, Mary Anna Randolph Custis Lee petitioned Congress for the return of Arlington to the family. A committee was formed. But the idea of Arlington as a national cemetery had begun to take hold, and Mary Lee's petition was soundly and thoroughly rejected.

The family eventually took the fight all the way to the Supreme Court, which found in the Lee family's favor on January 10, 1879. The court ordered fair value and restitution in dollars. George Washington Custis Lee, the oldest son of Mary and Robert, agreed to a payment of $150,000 and the matter was closed on April 24, 1883.

Today, the mansion at Arlington National Cemetery is the most visited historic house in the national park system. It receives about 650,000 visitors each year, and between one and two million people visit the grounds, according to park officials. It remains a focal point of the city and of the nation.

In July 2014, a $12.3 million dollar donation,

by David Rubenstein, a billionaire history buff and co-founder of The Carlyle Group, was dedicated to restoring the former slave quarters, the mansion, and the gardens.

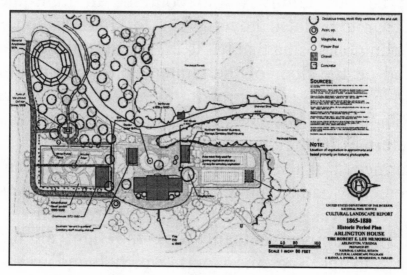

A current map of the Arlington House and surrounding grounds at Arlington National Cemetery.

Today, Arlington is harder to see from a metropolis that has grown exponentially from the days of antebellum Washington. However, when one looks westward, the proud columns still command attention on top of the hill. On sunlit mornings, the orange and yellow light pours down on the façade of the old mansion, as Washingtonians race to their cars, ready to do battle with the city's legendary traffic. And the house at the top of Arlington National Cemetery shines as a proud beacon to them all. It is a place of honor, service, and patriotism that all are proud of. It remains as it was in the days before the Civil War: the American Acropolis.

And on the grounds, in the spring and summer, roses and flowers grow in profusion. Many of the garden beds have been restored, with the help of historians, to recreate grounds as they might have looked more than 150 years ago, when Mary Anna Randolph Custis Lee nurtured them with her mother and sisters. One can still walk underneath the arbor or take a fragrant walk at dusk on those sacred grounds and walkways. Beautiful, colorful flowers.

And every Memorial Day, thousands of roses are placed on the innumerable white headstones around the cemetery to commemorate the ultimate sacrifice of those who have laid down their lives for this country.

Today Arlington House and Arlington National Cemetery together are one of the most visited of all the national parks in the United States.

ACKNOWLEDGMENTS

Any author of such an effort owes a great debt of gratitude to those who went before him. Several writers' works have proved invaluable, including Michael Korda, Douglass Southall Freeman, Clifford Dowdey, Elizabeth Brown Pryor, John Perry, Robert M. Poole, David W. Miller, and Mary A. Giunta, among many others. I would also like to thank those folks at Washington & Lee University and the archives at Arlington National Cemetery who were invaluable in their help.

Of course, I pored over more than five hundred original sources, including letters and interviews with Robert E. Lee, Mrs. Lee, Montgomery C. Meigs, and many others.

Special gratitude goes toward Mark Saloky, CTR, and Melissa of the Public Affairs Office, both of Arlington National Cemetery for all their help and advice and guidance. I am also incredibly indebted to Seth McCormick-Goodhart, Senior Special Collections Assistant, James G. Leyburn Library at Washington and Lee University. Without these individuals, this kind of work cannot be done.

As ever, I owe a debt of special thanks in all of my professional endeavors to Gilbert King for his ear, opinions, advice, general good cheer, and encouragement. Others who also cheered me on were Michael Fragnito and Caitlin Friedman among others.

I would, of course, like to thank John Whalen of Cider Mill Press, who helped make this book a reality. Were it not for his excitement, enthusiasm, and faith in me, I might have given up under the weight of this massive project. I also owe a huge debt of gratitude to editors Alex Smith, Emilia Pisani, Alex Lewis, Becky Maines, and many others who helped mold a rather large manuscript into readable shape.

I would like to thank my sons, Dylan and Dawson, whom I have taken too much time away from in order to pursue not only this work, but also my other professional aspirations. I have tried to attend as many of their events as possible, but there is no replacement for a catch or an evening's conversation, many of which were robbed by my other pursuits. I owe it to them to spend more time hanging out and less time working.

END NOTES

PROLOGUE: AMERICAN ACROPOLIS

"We proceeded along a perfect road through a Country . . . Poole, Robert M. *On Hallowed Ground: The Story of Arlington National Cemetery.* New York, N.Y.: Walker &, 2009. p. 68–69

CHAPTER 1: THE ROSE OF ARLINGTON

"Mary's earliest memories . . . Perry, John, and John Perry. *Mrs. Robert E. Lee: The Lady of Arlington.* Multnomah Publishers, 2003. p. 59

"As Mary began the transition from girl . . . Perry, p. 51

"Her most notable education . . . Pryor, Elizabeth Brown. Mary Anna Randolph Custis Lee, *Encyclopedia of Virginia.* http://www.encyclo pediavirginia.org/Lee_Mary_Anna_Randolph _Custis_1807-1873

"Custis also had a rich store of anecdotes . . . Pryor, *Encyclopedia of Virginia*

"descended from Virginia's notable families . . . Pryor, *Encyclopedia of Virginia*

"Taste may be defined as the power of . . . Perry, p. 51

"Her ability soon far surpassed her father's . . . Perry, p. 52

"combined to make her a toast . . . Perry, p. 52

"she was the girl the crowd gathered around . . . Perry, p. 56

"Congressman Houston crossed the Potomac . . . Perry, p. 57

"Mary was, evidently, an accomplished flirt . . . Pryor, Elizabeth Brown, and Robert E. Lee. *Reading the Man: A Portrait of Robert E. Lee through His Private Letters.* New York: Viking, 2007. p. 74

"In 1830, with the death of William Henry Fitzhugh . . . Pryor, *Encyclopedia of Virgina*

"So it was that two spirits came together in the summer of 1830 . . . Pryor, *Reading the Man*, p. 76

CHAPTER 2: ROBERT E. LEE

"The newly graduated honor student . . . Dowdey, Clifford. *Lee with Photographs and with Maps by Samuel H. Bryant.* Boston: Little, Brown, 1965. p. 47

"Lee's writings indicate he may . . . Pryor, *Encyclopedia of Virginia*

"Forty years ago I stood in this room . . . Dowdey, p. 47

That I alas must be of those . . . Pryor, *Reading the Man*, p. 77

"As she stopped over the Mount Vernon sideboard . . . Perry, p. 68

"something miraculous happened . . . Perry, p. 71

"He spoke of his delight in her person . . . Pryor, *Reading the Man*, p. 78

CHAPTER 3: MONTGOMERY C. MEIGS

"his intimate associations with Lieutenant Lee . . . Miller, David W. *Second Only to Grant: Quartermaster General Montgomery C. Meigs: A Biography*. Shippensburg, Pa.: White Mane Books, 2000. p. 13

Lee "went out with the civilian workers . . . Dowdey, p. 65.

"maintained and preserved under all circumstances . . . Miller, p. 13

CHAPTER 4: ROBERT E. LEE SAVES ARLINGTON

"I will do my best, she wrote to Lee . . . Korda, Michael. *Clouds of Glory: The Life and Legend of Robert E. Lee*. Harper, New York, NY, 2014. p. 198

"In the 1850s, when communications . . . Korda, p.198

"God have mercy on me in my last . . . Perry, p. 198

"In contrast to his wife's quiet, private funeral service . . . Perry, p. 199

"Newspapers throughout the country carried . . . Perry, p. 199

"Balding and undistinguished in appearance . . . Dowdey, p. 54

"The family's problems nearly overwhelmed . . . Korda, p. 198

"I almost dread his seeing my crippled state . . . Dowdey, p. 111

"He has left me an unpleasant legacy . . . Pryor, *Reading the Man*, p. 262

"There is no such provision . . . Pryor, p. 262

"Lee had interpreted the Custis will . . . Pryor, p. 265

"Lee went at the complex problem . . . Dowdey, p. 112–113

"However difficult it might be . . . Korda, p. 202

"Lee was never an enthusiast of slavery . . . Korda, p. 209

"You certainly look more like . . . Nelligan, Murray H. *Old Arlington: The Story of the Robert E. Lee Memorial.* Burke, VA: National Park Service Historical Handbook Series No. 6 ; Washington, D.C., 1950 (REVISED 1962)

"We had tea in the Washington teacups . . . Nelligan

"The flower garden was as important to the Lee family . . . Nelligan

"[We] found your grandfather at the . . . Nelligan

"I was very glad to receive, my Sweet Annie, your letter . . . Nelligan

CHAPTER 5: MEIGS AND THE GREAT DOME
"I found upon my table tonight a card . . . Meigs, Montgomery C., and Wendy Wolff.

158

Capitol Builder: The Shorthand Journals of Montgomery C. Meigs, 1853–1859, 1861: A Project to Commemorate the United States Capitol Bicentennial, 1800–2000. Washington, DC: U.S. G.P.O., 2001. p. 655

"John Lee called and told me that . . . Meigs, *Capitol Builder*, p. 655

"John Lee told Robert Lee something of the matter . . . Meigs, *Capitol Builder*, p. 655

"He did not like to take up the time . . . Meigs, *Capitol Builder*, p. 655–656

CHAPTER 6: FLEEING ARLINGTON

"It was on Sunday, the 14th of April 1861, that . . . Pryor, Elizabeth Brown. "Thou Knowist Not The Time of Thy Visitation," *Virginia Magazine of History and Biography*, Vol. 119, No. 3. p. 289

"On Thursday, the 18th, He drove over to Washington . . . Pryor, "Thou Knowist," p. 289

"I remember him saying to me subsequently . . . Pryor, "Thou Knowist," p. 289

He had told Blair that, ". . . though opposed . . . Dowdey, p. 133

"Lee, you have made the greatest mistake . . . Dowdey, p. 133

Letter to Gen. Winfield Scott . . . Civil War Trust, http://www.civilwar.org/education/history /primarysources/letter-from-robert-e-lee-to.html

"He read from the rough draft . . . Dowdey, p. 133

"That same afternoon, a cousin . . . Pryor, "Thou Knowist," p. 289

"The Secession of Virginia was known now . . . Pryor, "Thou Knowist," p. 291

"My husband has wept tears of blood . . . Dowdey, p. 135

"About the same time, he had a revealing . . . Perry, p. 223

"As I was going out of town, one . . . Perry, p. 224

"I am very anxious about you . . . Perry, p. 224

"You had better prepare all things for removal . . . Perry, p. 224

"You've got to get out now . . . Perry, p. 224

"Beginning her preparations at last . . . Perry, p. 225

"The spring weather had been unusually . . . Perry, p. 226

"I never saw the countryside more beautiful . . . Perry, p. 227

"I am glad to hear you are at peace . . . Perry, p. 229

"And on a beautiful morning in the idle of May, 1861 . . . Perry, p. 229

CHAPTER 7: ARLINGTON GONE

"Maimed and wounded . . . http://www.nps.gov /arho/historyculture/cemetery.htm

"The private's grave was situated . . . Poole, p. 58

"an act of improvisation born of necessity . . . Poole, p. 58

"Incurred the ill will . . . Brigadier General, Montgomery C. Meigs, 14th Quartermaster General, May 1861–February 1882, US Army Quartermaster Foundation, Fort Lee, Virginia http://www.qmfound.com/BG_Montgomery _Meigs.htm

"Former Army comrades who had . . . Poole, p. 24

"No man who ever took the oath . . . Miller, p. 95

"Meigs responded . . . Rolfe, Steve. Montgomery C. Meigs, An Icon of the Civil War, *The Sentinel*, November, 2010, Monroe County Civil War Roundtable, Bloomington, IN, http://www.mccwrt-in.org/user%20submissions /Meigs.pdf

Montgomery's "soul seems to be on fire with indignation . . . Miller, p. 95

Meigs wrote himself, as "a great and holy war . . . Miller, p. 95

"Congress [to] pass a law banishing [the rebel] leaders . . . Miller, p. 253

"Meigs's reconstruction attitude was . . . Miller, p. 255

"Stanton, a Washington lawyer from the Midwest . . . Dowdey, p. 187

"The dreadful . . . Hearn, Chester G., *The Impeachment of Andrew Johnson*, McFarland & Publishers, Jefferson, North Carolina, 2000, p. 21

"The two men were often at variance . . . Allen Nevins, *The War for the Union: War Becomes*

Revolution, 1862–1863, Scribner, 1962, p. 35

Stanton's "arbitrary temper was accentuated . . . Nevins, p. 35

The Republican press hailed the choice . . . Poole, p. 62

"Meigs visited the new cemetery on the morning . . . Poole, p. 62

"Once Meigs had his new bureaucratic arrangements . . . Poole, p. 63

"Then went about encircling . . . The Revenge of Montgomery C. Meigs, *Main Line Today*, July 2014, http://www.mainlinetoday.com/Main -Line-Today/July-2014/The-Revenge-of -Montgomery-C-Meigs/

CHAPTER 8: DEATH COMES

"When words failed to stop his fighting with . . . Meigs, John Rodgers. *A Civil War Soldier of Christ and Country.* Edited by Mary A. Giunta. Chicago, IL: University of Illinois Press, 2006. p. 2

"Several important political leaders . . . Giunta, p. 2

"In early September 1859, Captain Montgomery C. Meigs . . . Giunta, p. 2

"On the death of Lieutenant Craig, Cadet Meigs . . . Schott, Robert Nicholson, U.S. War Department. *The War of Rebellion: A Compilation of the Official Records of the Union and Confederate Armies*, Washington, Government Printing Office, 1880, p. 380

"John is known as the Lieut General. Hand full of . . . Giunta, p. 235

"I should think that it would be rather cool . . . Giunta, p. 238

"Before I got to bed I must acknowledge . . . Giunta, p. 240

"What I saw there is burned into my memory . . . *National Park Service, The Burning—Cedar Creek and Belle Grove*, http://www.nps.gov /cebe/historyculture/the-burning.htm

"The father worried," wrote Montgomery C. Meigs's . . . Miller, p. 295

"On the morning of October 3, 1864, . . . Kaylor, Peter Cline. *The Killing of Lieutenant Meigs, 1864*, University of Texas, 1925

"Shaver, born and reared on the . . . Kaylor

"Shaver had never met Martin and Campbell . . . Kaylor

"Sheridan had believed that Meigs had fallen victim . . . Tucker, Spenser C., Editor, *American Civil War Encyclopedia*, Westport, CT, Greenwood, 2013, p. 1254

"Stanton came to the Meigs' home . . . Miller, p. 241

"About this hour my son, 1st Lt. John Rodgers Meigs . . . Giunta, p. 241

"much consolation in the memory of good deeds . . . Giunta, p. 242

"And so perishes my first born a noble boy . . . Giunta, p. 243

"Meigs' father believed that his . . . Pierpaoli

"The following day residents of Dayton . . . Kaylor

"After the war, the three Confederates . . . Pierpaoli, Paul G. Jr. *Montgomery Meigs, Biographical Dictionary of the Union*, Edited by John Hubbell, James W. Geary and Jon L. Wakelyn, Westport, CT, Greenwood Press, 1995

"One of the youngest and brightest . . . Miller, p. 242

"When I look back over the years . . . Giunta, p. 244

"his consequent embitterment sealed . . . Montgomery C. Meigs, Editors Hubbell, John; Geary, James W.; and Wakelyn, Jon L., *Biographical Dictionary of the Union*, Westport, CT, Greenwood, 1995

CHAPTER 9: SEARCHING FOR ARLINGTON

"Mary lost no time in applying . . . Perry, p. 287

"After a warm welcome, the Lee family . . . Perry, p. 288

"My heart yearns to be . . . Perry, p. 291

"But time passed, and with it . . . Perry, p. 290

"she was always bright, sunny-tempered . . . Perry, p. 290

"I expect to join my husband . . . Lee, Mary Custis, Letters, Washington & Lee University, November 23, 1865

"Despite every effort to speed . . . Korda, p. 684

"Although they were much too . . . Korda, p. 684

"I hope the possessors . . . Lee, Robert E.,
Recollections and Letters of Robert E. Lee,
Dover Publications, 1977

"My cousin, Miss Heather Williams . . . Lee, Mary
Custis, Letters, Washington & Lee University,
September 12, 1866

"I have been hoping . . . Lee, Mary Custis, Letters,
Washington & Lee University, October 12,
1866

"Upon reflection I have . . . Lee, Mary Custis,
Letters, Washington & Lee University,
Novermber 12, 1866

"I am still confined mostly to my . . . Perry, p. 305

CHAPTER 10: THE TOMB OF THE
UNKNOWN SOLDIER

"It is thought well for persons who . . . Poole,
p. 66

"I cannot write with composure . . . Poole, p. 66

"Among Lee's adversaries, no one seemed . . .
Poole, p. 65

"The rebels are all murderers of my son . . . Poole,
p. 65

"The Quartermaster General . . . Poole, p. 72

"To underscore the urgency . . . The Beginnings
of Arlington National Cemetery, National
Parks Service, http://www.nps.gov/arho/history
culture/cemetery.htm

Selected Bibliography

Coulling, Mary P. *The Lee Girls.* Winston-Salem, N.C.: J.F. Blair, 1987.

Craven, Avery. "To Markie," *The Letters of Robert E. Lee to Martha Custis Williams.* Boston, MA: Harvard University Press, 1934.

deButts, Mary Custis Lee. ed. *Growing Up in the 1850s: The Journal of Agnes Lee.* Chapel Hill, NC: The University of North Carolina Press, 1984.

Dowdey, Clifford. *Lee with Photographs and with Maps by Samuel H. Bryant.* Boston: Little, Brown, 1965.

Faust, Drew Gilpin. *This Republic of Suffering: Death and the American Civil War.* New York: Alfred A. Knopf, 2008.

Flower, Frank. *Edwin McMaster Stanton.* New York: Saalfield Publishing, 1905.

Freeman, Douglass Southall. *Lee: An Abridgement*, Edited by Richard Harwell, Scribners, New York, NY, 1961.

Jones, J. William. *Personal Reminiscences of General Robert E. Lee.* Richmond, Va.: United States Historical Society Press, 1989.

Kaylor, Peter Cline. *The Killing of Lieutenant Meigs, 1864.* University of Texas, 1925.

Korda, Michael. *Clouds of Glory: The Life and*

Legend of Robert E. Lee. Harper, New York, NY, 2014.

Robert E. Lee Papers, Coll. 0064, Special Collections, Leyburn Library, Washington and Lee University, Lexington, VA from the WLU Collection #0170 of the Lee-Jackson Foundation Collection and WLU's Lee Family Digital Archive.

Lee, Robert E., and Clifford Dowdey. *The Wartime Papers of R.E. Lee.* Boston: Little, Brown, 1961.

Long, A. L., and Marcus J. Wright. *Memoirs of Robert E. Lee: His Military and Personal History, Embracing a Large Amount of Information Hitherto Unpublished.* Secaucus, N.J.: Blue and Grey Press, 1983.

Meigs, John Rodgers. *A Civil War Soldier of Christ and Country.* Edited by Mary A. Giunta. Chicago, IL: University of Illinois Press, 2006.

Meigs, Montgomery C., and Wendy Wolff. *Capitol Builder: The Shorthand Journals of Montgomery C. Meigs, 1853–1859, 1861: A Project to Commemorate the United States Capitol Bicentennial, 1800–2000.* Washington, DC: U.S. G.P.O., 2001.

Miller, David W. *Second Only to Grant: Quartermaster General Montgomery C. Meigs: A Biography.* Shippensburg, Pa.: White Mane Books, 2000.

Nagel, Paul C. *The Lees of Virginia: Seven Generations of an American Family.* New York: Oxford University Press, 1990.

Nelligan, Murray H. *Old Arlington: The Story of the Robert E. Lee Memorial,* Burke, VA: National Park Service Historical Handbook Series No. 6 ; Washington, D.C., 1950 (REVISED 1962).

Nevins, Allen. *The War for the Union: War Becomes Revolution, 1862–1863,* New York, NY, Charles Scribner and Sons, 1960.

Peters, James Edward. *Arlington National Cemetery.* Bethesda, MD: Woodbine House, 2008.

Perry, John, and John Perry. *Mrs. Robert E. Lee: The Lady of Arlington.* Multnomah Publishers, 2003.

Pierpaoli, Paul G. Jr. *Montgomery Meigs, Biographical Dictionary of the Union,* Edited by John Hubbell, James W. Geary and Jon L. Wakelyn, Westport, CT, Greenwood Press, 1995.

Poole, Robert M. *On Hallowed Ground: The Story of Arlington National Cemetery.* New York, N.Y.: Walker &, 2009.

Pryor, Elizabeth Brown, and Robert E. Lee. *Reading the Man: A Portrait of Robert E. Lee through His Private Letters.* New York: Viking, 2007.

Pryor, Elizabeth Brown. "Thou Knowist Not The

Time of Thy Visitation", *Virginia Magazine of History and Biography*, Vol. 119, No. 3. p. 276–296.

Stanton, Edwin McMasters. The War in Georgia, *Dispatch War Department*, October 7, 1864.

Thomas, Benjamin P., and Harold M. Hyman. *Stanton: The Life and Times of Lincoln's Secretary of War.* New York, NY: Alfred A. Knopf, 1962.

Tucker, Spenser C., Editor. *American Civil War Encyclopedia*, Westport, CT, Greenwood, 2013.

Photo Credits

Pages 16, 20, 21, 37, 38, 41, 43, 44, 46, 56, 59, 60, 62–63, 64, 76, 77, 93, 94, 97, 102, 108, 121, 122, 134, 138, 139, and 152 are reprinted courtesy of the Library of Congress

Pages 30, 119, 125, 131, and 148 are all reprinted courtesy of GNU Free Documentation License, Creative Commons c/o Wikipedia

Pages 45, 92, 138, 145, 146, and 150 are all used courtesy of the National Parks Service and Arlington Cemetery

Page 55 Arlington National Cemetery, reprinted under license from Shutterstock.com

Page 118 Historical Marker Database courtesy of Bernard Fisher, December 27, 2008

Page 133 courtesy of The Museum of the American Revolution, Philadelphia, PA

About the Author

Carlo DeVito is a lifelong publishing executive with more than 20 years experience. He has published books with Stephen Hawking, E.O. Wilson, Arthur M. Schlesinger Jr., Dan Rather, Philip Caputo, Michael Lewis, James McPherson, Gilbert King, Cay Risen, Peter Kaminisky, Thomas Hoving, David Margolick, Stanley Crouch, John Edgar Wideman, Dee Brown, Julia Alvarez, Jane Goodall, Budd Schulberg, Haynes Johnson, Malachy McCourt, David Quammen, Peter Golenbock, The Fabulous Beekman Boys, Barton Seaver, Kevin Zraly, Matt Kramer, Terry Walters, and many others.

Carlo DeVito is the author of more than 15 titles. He has written on dogs, sports, and wine. He has appeared on television dozens of times including multiple times as guests on CBS, ABC, NBC, and FOX morning shows in New York, as well as throughout the eastern seaboard. He has been a featured guest on WFAN (both TV and Radio), ESPN radio, WCBS and WABC radio, WAMC, and more than 60 radio stations nationwide. He has edited and written more than a dozen books reviewed in *The Wall Street Journal*, *USA Today*, *The Hartford Courant*, *The*

Christian Science Monitor, and other national newspapers.

His most recent titles include *A Mark Twain Christmas: A Journey Across Three Christmas Seasons*; *Inventing Scrooge: The Incredible True Story Behind Charles Dickens' Legendary "A Christmas Carol"*; and edited *Mark Twain's Notebooks: Journals, Letters, Observations, Wit, Wisdom, and Doodles*.

He publishes a highly-acclaimed wine blog, East Coast Wineries, and is owner of the Hudson-Chatham Winery, in Ghent, NY, where he lives with his family.

Center Point Large Print
600 Brooks Road / PO Box 1
Thorndike, ME 04986-0001 USA

(207) 568-3717

US & Canada:
1 800 929-9108
www.centerpointlargeprint.com